ADAM'S ADVENTURE

Walking In the Footsteps of History in His Hometown: New Bern, North Carolina

By:

Charlotte Truette

PublishAmerica
Baltimore

Hardcover 9781462662760
Softcover 9781462676309
PUBLISHED BY PUBLISHAMERICA, LLLP
www.publishamerica.com
Baltimore

Printed in the United States of America

DEDICATION

To Dr. Staley Moore and Dr. Kimberly Livingston, their proactive medical care and innovative medical procedures made this all possible.

Because they taught him how to read, Adam wishes to thank and include: Wanda Spinner Powers, Paul Powers, Nelson MacDonald, and his teachers at Vanceboro Farm Life Elementary School: Mrs. Thomas, Mrs. Wooten, Mrs. Allen, and Mrs. Fields

Table of Contents

PART I:
ADAM'S ADVENTURE INTO HISTORY SENDS HIM ON SEVEN JOURNEYS

The First Journey is by Book,
Reading about the Old Times

They Didn't Know About Gravity Either

"Boring, boorriinngg, booorrriiinnnggg!" wailed Adam, his voice tone rising louder with each word, as he twirled around and around the living room, in ever-larger circles, before collapsing onto the sofa.

Lying on his back, waving his hands in the air for emphasis, Adam cried out, "And it's not even true! None of that even happened!" Then, in obvious disgust and disbelief, he let his arms fall to his sides and closed his eyes appearing as if he had fainted because it was all just too much to bear.

Nana, chuckling to herself, quickly explained, "Okay, Adam, we can take out the 'booorrriiinnnggg' details because they might slow down the story in our book, but they might not be boring to everyone. Maybe we could have a 'boring to Adam but interesting to Nana details section' in the back of our book."

"Okay," replied Adam, "but I'm not reading that part of the book."

"Okay," Nana agreed, adding "but we do want our book to be a true story about your adventure into history, right?"

"Correct," confirmed Adam, explaining, "Nana I didn't say 'right' because I like to say the word 'correct'. I like the way it sounds when I say it," saying correct again with an emphasis on the last syllable.

"Correct is probably a better word this time because 'right' can mean other things: Like in the United States Bill of Rights. You wouldn't say the United States Bill of Corrects, right?" asked Nana, keeping the word game going.

"Correct," agreed Adam, emphasizing the first syllable this time.

Still playing along Nana replied, "You got that right!" causing Adam to laugh so he could barely whisper "Correct!" one last time.

"Adam we have to know where to go if we want to walk in an adventurer's footsteps. I got some of the ideas for your adventure from stories in our library books," explained Nana.

"A lot happened around here and when you read the books I know you will have some great adventure ideas too.

"Since we want to write a history book, we should research New Bern's history and search for personal and eyewitness stories because we want to know people's version of what happened. The exciting part about doing our own research is that we know many things today that they didn't know we know how things turned out for them and what happened after they died."

Knowing how much Adam liked pretending and planning adventures Nana added, "But before we can go on your adventure into history we have to make adventure plans first."

At the mention of 'adventure plans' Adam jumped of the sofa, to sit on the floor facing Nana. "We can walk Indian file and pretend we're Indians," suggested Adam.

"I like that idea a lot Adam. The whole point of walking Indian file is to step into the exact footsteps left by the ones who went before and I know where to buy us some real deerskin moccasins we can wear when we go adventuring.

"Adam you're lucky that you live in such an important historical region. This is where the United States and Carolina's history began. We can even see artifacts that the adventurers left behind including some that belonged to Blackbeard. Just a few years ago, they found Blackbeard's wrecked ship, the Queen Anne's Revenge (QAR) that he sank about 7 years after the founding of New Bern."

"Nana if we're celebrating New Bern's 300th birthday that means the QAR was under water for almost 300 years before anyone found it?" questioned Adam, somewhat in disbelief that the story about Blackbeard sinking his ship was not just another pretend pirate movie.

"Blackbeard's ship was found not far from here in Beaufort Inlet near Fort Macon. Some of the things found with the QAR are on display in a Beaufort museum we can visit.

"How about this idea Adam, because historians can't write down everything there's a lot of stories about what happened around Carolina's inner and outer banks that you might not read about in many history books. We can include some of them in our book and plan adventure journeys to follow them.

For example, we could plan a journey by water and follow the Indians, explorers, adventurers, slaves, pirates, and German submarines and go to that museum in Beaufort."

Eager to begin, Adam said, "I'd love that Nana, when can we go?"

"Soon, but Adam your adventure into history makes me wonder what our Baron might say if he knew that three hundred years after he founded New Bern people would write books about his American adventure and New Bern would become an important destination for anyone who wanted to take a trip into the past.

"Or what Blackbeard might say if he knew that because he wrecked the QAR in Beaufort Inlet it would help the city of Beaufort, North Carolina become a favorite tourist destination?"

"I'm glad he wrecked it nearby Nana. I never though I would ever get to see anything that belonged to Blackbeard."

"Isn't it wonderful how history can show how one thing leads to another resulting in totally unsuspected consequences and reaching far into the future? Don't forget all of these people are real."

"And dead!" declared Adam.

"True, you will see a lot of dead people," Nana replied. "What do you think about this idea; we can pretend we are two tourists and we came here on vacation because we love history and we'll plan on having a lot of fun. Will that work for you, Adam?"

"Yes ma'am! I'll make plans we'll really like!" Adam said with enthusiasm, warming up to the idea of an adventure that included real pirates.

"Just be careful it's not too adventurous Adam, I'm not a tomboy anymore, but first are you ready to go time traveling by book?" asked Nana; while spreading five books out upon the living room floor in a wide semi-circle, in front of Adam.

"Okay," Adam agreed. "But don't forget about the boring section."

"Okay, I won't, but remember you need to let me know when you think a detail is boring," Nana warned.

"We should start with first things first and learn about New Bern's history before it was New Bern," suggested Nana. "Life moves forward but we have to go back in time and start at the very beginning if we really want to understand history and see the truth, because it's only the big picture that truthfully reveals who is who, what is what, and how one thing leads to another."

Through Indian Eyes

Opening a very large book, *Through Indian Eyes*, Adam slowly turned the pages as Nana began telling him the stories behind the pictures.

"Sir Walter Raleigh's first explorers came here and reported to him they had 'discovered a paradise world full of everything' where the natives lived in the 'most pleasant and plentiful places in the whole world'.

"In those days Native American Indians lived in small villages spread out along the banks of the rivers and streams that some claimed had more fish than water in them.

"Even though Indians didn't have guns or horses they could kill with their bows and arrows and their canoes could take them to most of the places they wanted to go because the rivers and streams were their roads.

"Families lived together and cared for one another and the families grouped together making a village and making new villages as the number of families grew, but they were all bound together as a tribe who spoke the same language. If you think about it Adam, speaking the same language still has that same power to bind people together.

"Even though their vocabulary was very small in comparison to our vocabulary their common language gave them the power of communication and most tribes lived together in a democratic way. Which means the Indians agreed on who would be their chief and everyone had a say at tribal counsels and anyone could debate on anything that was important, and all contributed in their own way to the wellbeing of the whole tribe.

"Generally, tribes had many chiefs; the peace chief would be the most important during peace, and during wars it would be the war chief, who had to be good at planning and fighting.

They would also have a planting chief, and other experts who would oversee different activities and events. In fact, there's a famous saying 'to many chiefs and not enough Indians' that shows just how things can get out of hand, so there always had to be the head chief who would make the final decisions.

"Some archeologists believe Native Indians have lived around this area for at least10, 000 years but during all of those thousands of years the Indians had never known real trouble.

"About the only trouble they had were occasional wars with neighboring tribes, when someone wanted revenge, which of course was bad enough.

"I guess you could say that real trouble first arrived in the New World with Christopher Columbus.

"Adam, Columbus and his three ships would be the first to sail out of sight of land into the Western Ocean," then, dipping her head to catch Adam's attention, she added "on purpose."

Nana explained, "In those days the Atlantic Ocean was named the Western Ocean on maps and less than half of the world had been discovered. No one even imagined that the North or South American continents or the Pacific Ocean even existed. Some people still thought the world was flat and the horizon was the edge of the world. That you would fall off the earth if you sailed to far from shore."

Laughing, Adam picked up a chessboard and moving his hands around it as if he were sailing an imaginary ship around an imaginary, flat world he declared "Then they didn't know anything about gravity either. You can't fall off of the world Nana gravity wouldn't let you, even if the world was flat!"

Wanda, Adam's mom, an elementary school teacher added, "Nana's right Adam. We can laugh now because we know about gravity, in 1492 most people thought things fell to earth because earth was the center of the universe. It was almost two hundred years later before Isaac Newton published his theory about gravity.

"We take many important things for grant today that early explorers didn't know about or didn't have. For instance, the telescope was invented in1608; that would be 116 years after Columbus and 24 years after Raleigh's explorers came to the New World.

"They also didn't know the Earth's circumference at the Equator is 24,901.55 miles or that the oceans were so big.

"Columbus first tried to get King John II to fund his exploration and he estimated the distance from Portugal to China would be 2,400 miles but the king's experts thought that was to low so Portugal refused to fund it, that's why he had to ask Spain to fund his attempt to reach the Orient."

Catching Adam's attention with such unexpected news, Wanda continued, "Adam, not only did they worry about falling off a flat world, they worried about endless whirlpools that could swallow ships. That they might sail into areas of boiling hot water that would cook anything that came near it. But worst of all, that giant sea monsters were waiting to eat them, ship and all, in one big gulp," making Adam laugh when she grabbed him, pretending to be a giant sea-monster.

"Oh, there's no doubt about it Adam, those first explorers had to be brave and courageous. We cannot really imagine what they must have gone through but we can understand why they would want to give up," said Nana.

"A sailor's life was hard. Ships could only carry a few months of food and water so it had to be carefully rationed; and, if the weather was good, one hot meal a day.

"Columbus had underestimated the circumference of the earth by 37% and he thought it would only take four weeks to reach China. After being surrounded by endless water for a month the sailors wanted to turn around and go back home.

"In his journal, Columbus tells about how it became harder and harder for him to keep the crew going as the days turned into weeks and by the fifth week the sailors threatened mutiny.

"Columbus didn't really know how far they would have to travel from Spain, or that it would take so long before they would reach land and get more water and food, but he knew in his heart that the earth was round so he refused to give up and return to Spain.

"On October 7th his crew saw birds and Columbus changed course to follow them.

"By October 10th, his crew was once again on the verge of munity and demanding to return to Spain. Columbus tried to motivate them to overcome their fears by reminding them of the reward of a lifetime pension promised by King Ferdinand and Queen Isabella to the first one to spot land, and promised to return to Spain if they had not reached land in three days.

"They had sailed about 4,100 miles when a lookout on the Pinta spotted land around 2 a.m. on the morning of October 12, 1492 and the captain fired one of his ship's cannons as the agreed way of telling the good news to Columbus, who was on the Santa Maria. Later, Columbus claimed the pension for himself, saying he had spotted land first, because he had seen a light from the campfire on the shore a few hours earlier.

"Adam, the purpose of Columbus's voyage was to find a new way to reach Asia in order to buy spices. People traveled to the ends of the earth and risked their lives to find spices, to flavor their foods and to make medicines, and for salt.

"Today salt is cheap and easy to get but back then people needed salt to preserve food and it was so hard to get that it was as valuable as gold.

"Columbus had only been gone 7 ½ months when he returned to Spain a hero on March 15, 1493. He did not bring back any spices, but brought back what he had found, including a few Indians he had kidnapped, hoping Spain would do like Portugal and setup a slave trade but they refused. He also brought back a little bit of gold, tobacco plants, pineapples, turkeys, chili peppers, and hammocks."

"Hammocks that you tie between two trees," quizzed Adam.

"Yes, I researched hammocks and learned that the origins of the hammock go back 1000 years and was invented in Central America by the Mayan Indians. Trading had spread their use to other areas, so that by the time Columbus arrived in the New World the Natives living on the islands around Bermuda were using them," Nana replied.

"It didn't take long before news that Columbus had discovered a new world spread like a wildfire across Europe and soon real trouble was on the way and it would change everything for the Indians," Nana said. "First in South America, then, about ninety years later, real trouble would come here Adam, sent because of a queen's gift.

"Her gift is a Charter, given on March 25, 1584, and I want to read the first part of it out-loud for you, it begins:

"Elizabeth, by the grace of God of England, France, and Ireland, Queen, defender of the faith &c. To all people to whom these presents shall come, greetings. Know ye that of our especial grace, certain science, & mere motion, we have given and granted, and by these presents for us, our heirs and successors do give and grant to our trusty and well-beloved servant Walter Raleigh Esquire, and to his heirs and assigns for ever, free liberty & license from time to time, and at all times forever hereafter, to discover, search, find out, and view such remote, heathen and barbarous lands, countries, and territories, not actually possessed of any Christian prince, nor inhabited by Christian people, as to him, his heirs and assigns, and to every or any of them shall seem good, and the same to have, hold, occupy & enjoy to him, his heirs and assigns for ever, with all prerogatives, commodities, jurisdictions, royalties, privileges, franchises and preeminence, thereto or thereabouts both by sea and land, whatsoever we by our letters patents may grant..."

Gods on Floating Islands Bring Real Trouble

Nana slid the book, *Adventures To A New World*, closer to Adam saying, "Four hundred and twenty seven years ago only Native American Indians lived here when Raleigh's explorers arrived and the Indians knew nothing about the Old World.

"They knew nothing about England or Queen Elizabeth I or that she had given away their land to her favorite courtier Walter Raleigh."

Adam asked "Nana, what does 'courtier' mean?"

"A courtier is often at the court of a queen or other royal, like a king or a prince, and tries to win their favor by using flattery and charm and Raleigh was very charming.

"Right away, Raleigh sent the first English explorers on a reconnaissance mission to lay claim for the land and to select the perfect location for his first colony.

"They left England on April 27, 1584 and they arrived on July 4, 1584 on Carolina's outer banks and made a base on Roanoke Island. From there they explored up and down all of the rivers and creeks around here and they drew for Raleigh the very first map of Carolina's inner and outer banks and the location of different Indian tribes and their villages.

"The map shows the location of two of the Neusiok Indian villages on the Neuse River. One is where New Bern would be

126 years later and the other one appears to be where Cherry Point Marine Base would be 355 years later.

"Adam we know what those Indians looked like because on the second trip Raleigh sent an artist, John White, to record their discoveries. We can see them on this website," said Nana, as she typed the address: http://www.nps.gov/fora/photosmultimedia/johnwhitewatercolors.

Nana explained; "This is the internet site for the United States Department of the Interior National Park Service at Fort Raleigh on Roanoke Island. It says that the British Museum has given them permission to show John White's watercolors.

"The Indians in these watercolors are of the people Raleigh's explorers met when they first came here. The explorers said the Indians thought the explorers were Gods on floating islands and that the ship's sails were clouds that carried them from the sky to earth.

"This one is a drawing of a Pamlico Indian chief's wife and their daughter."

"Nana, it says she's about 9 or 10 years old!" exclaimed Adam, somewhat amazed at seeing a real Indian girl.

"Her tribe lived just across the Neuse River in Pamlico County. My guess is that they lived near the main Indian trading post, somewhere around Minnesott Beach or Oriental.

"She's posing for this picture so there's no doubt that she knows John White and since here father is the head Chief of the Pamlico Indians she probably knew Manteo and most all of the other important people who came here during those days.

"Looking at this picture of her holding out a doll, it seems as if she's saying 'look at this present I got from the Gods'. You wouldn't be able to guess that she'll soon be witnessing real trouble, a calamity that will change life for her and her tribe forever."

Clicking on the close button Nana said, "Let's sit back down on the floor I want to show you some other pictures from those days."

Picking up one of the books, *THE HISTORY AND ROMANCE OF EXPLORATION TOLD WITH PICTURE*, she opened it to a marked page and said, "Take a good look at these pictures Adam, some are of the explorers the Indians mistook for Gods and we can see from the huge sails on the tall ships why they thought they were clouds."

Pointing to one of the pictures Adam asked, "Who is Sir Francis Drake?"

"Drake was a relative and friend of Raleigh's and one of England's most famous explorers. You'll learn about him in school, but I'll tell you a story about when he came here.

"Adam, you already know a privateer is a legal pirate for his ruler, and that he plunders his ruler's enemies but doesn't keep the plunder. Privateers gave the plunder to their ruler, who then rewards them for their service.

"Drake and Raleigh were both successful privateers and the Queen was very generous with her rewards, giving them dozens of captured ships and generous shares of the plunder, and they both became very rich.

"Drake was on his way back to England when he decided to come to Roanoke Island to check on Raleigh's first colony. He had 23 ships carrying six hundred men and shiploads of plunder that was mostly Spanish gold.

"When Drake learned the colony was starving, because it had gotten its self into a big mess with the Indians, he wanted to help them.

"The colony accepted Drake's first offer, to give them ships, men, and food so that they could stay on Roanoke Island but before Drake left a hurricane hit and the ships Drake gave them were lost in the hurricane. Drake offered to give them more ships and supplies, or they could come with him to England. The colony decided to accept Drake's offer and went back to England.

"The explorers tell about it in reports to Raleigh, which are the first written accounts of a hurricane here. They tell how Drake and his ships had been in more danger of sinking on the dangerous shoals along our coast during the hurricane than he had ever been from the Spanish.

"Adam, can you imagine what the Indians must have thought when they saw one of England's most famous explorers, with his fleet of 23 ships armed with cannons and six hundred men armed with guns and swords?

"Or what they must have though when his fleet sails for England and the settlers go with him?"

"I imagine the Indians would have been scared when they saw all of those big ships because Indians just had little canoes, and I imagine that they were probably so happy to see them leave that they had a celebration!" declared Adam with conviction.

"There is no doubt that the Indians were glad to see them leave," agreed Nana. "But I do not believe that Raleigh was glad to see them back in England.

"Do you want to hear about how Raleigh sold his Roanoke colony to the leaders of the colony and why, just a couple of years later, it became the 'Lost Colony'? And why Raleigh went to prison for love and again later for treason and how he lost both Virginia and his head?"

Real Trouble Is Ahead For Raleigh

"Adam, even though Raleigh never came here, North Carolina's capital was named Raleigh to honor him.

"Oh, there's no doubt Raleigh wanted to personally explore his gift of land in the New World because he was a real-life adventurer and explorer, but the queen wouldn't let him.

"There's a story told on England's royal website about why there's a cape shown on Raleigh's coat of arms.

"One day, as the queen and her entourage were out for a walk a large mud puddle blocked her way.

"Raleigh was nearby and immediately removed his expensive cape and flung it out over the mud so she could cross over the mud puddle without getting her slippers dirty. As I said, Raleigh could be very charming.

"After the discovery of Virginia the queen knighted Raleigh and of course a knight needs a coat-of-arms and Raleigh designed his with a cape on it.

Back then, under the feudal system, the Crown owned all of the land in the kingdom's realm, no matter where it was, and her gift made Raleigh a Lord Proprietor, with an exclusive opportunity to develop real estate. The queen expected the northern part of the New World would pay off big for her, like the southern part was doing for Spain, and she reserved for the Crown a fifth of any gold and silver that was discovered and there was a stipulation giving him seven years to establish a colony.

"Raleigh also expected to make a lot of money, someday. First, he had to get his real estate development carved out of the wilderness, and that was not going to be cheap or easy, but both of Raleigh's colonies in Virginia failed Adam.

"Instead of the explores and settlers living as equal friends and neighbors with the Indians who welcomed them with love and help, the settlers committed terrible blunders that had serious consequences, so that soon there was real trouble for everyone, especially for the Indians.

"I read the reports to Raleigh telling how one of Raleigh's relatives, Sir Grenville, personally led one of the attacks against the Indians. Not only did they tear down and set fire to all of the huts in their village, Aquascogoc, but they also ruined their gardens and killed the Indians living there, including women and children. They said they let a few run away so they would scare other Indians when they told them what happened to them.

"They had killed a chief and almost everyone else living in the village because one of the villagers had taken a silver goblet from their ship.

"Of course, bows and arrows are no match for guns and the Indians suffered from other deadly incidents, fighting with Raleigh's men.

"The 'invisible bullets' were just as deadly for the Indians; that's the name Indians gave the germs causing measles and smallpox that the settlers brought with them to the New World.

"There is also real trouble headed for England, war is coming between England and Spain, and the queen is counting on Raleigh and his ships, and those of his friends and relatives, like Drake, to protect England from the Spanish Armada.

"Raleigh's colony is about 3,700 miles away from England and, because the queen refuses to let Raleigh leave England, Raleigh has to rely on others.

"They did defeat the Spanish Armada and saved England, Adam, but things did not go well for Raleigh's colony because the ones he counted on let him down.

"Now it seems that everything could have been a lot better if everyone had followed instructions and directions given by the Queen, to treat the Indians well, and by Raleigh, to settle the second colony in the Chesapeake Bay area instead of on Roanoke Island.

"Some say his second attempt failed because Raleigh's enemies prevented him from sending supplies and more people with John White to rescue the colony on Roanoke Island, causing the second colony to become the 'Lost Colony'.

"Adam, I tried to summarize all that information to help you understand why things happened as they did. Remember I did try to read you the reports Raleigh's men wrote."

"Yes, I do remember banishing all of that to the boring section Nana; so please don't make me do it again," pleaded Adam, with a pained look on his face.

"I think we should at least add some clues for readers to follow," said Nana.

"Nana I think it will be funny if we don't mention where the clues are," Adam said. "Then readers will be surprised when they find one."

"Okay," agreed Nana. "But we don't want to irritate our readers by causing their research to be troublesome, researching history and trying to interpret the stories it tells should be exciting."

Glad Nana agreed to hide some of the clues, Adam replied, "And I don't want to irritate readers either Nana that's why I banish the boring parts, and there's been so many that the boring section might be longer than the part about my actual adventure into history."

"It will be if you don't stop banishing them," laughed Nana. "Although to tell the truth taking out some of the stuff you though was boring will help edit our book because a lot of boring details can slow down a good story. Don't you agree though that we have to include some information, after all our readers deserve to know how we reached our conclusions, then if they want to know more they can read the boring details."

"I know Nana, and you've already done a lot of that," accused Adam. "I let it pass so the reader could learn something because some of New Bern's history can be boring when you first learn about it, but later, when you go somewhere on an adventure and remember the boring details, they can become interesting, or at least some of them do."

"Well said and I agree Adam," Nana replied. "However, I think you'll find this part is very interesting because crimes and criminals leave trails, like a slimy snail.

"I've been using the internet to research the colonial records that reveal some important back-stories about the history of your hometown.

"My research included following paper trails that lead to real estate deeds and surveys, letters, and official communications from queens and kings, Carolina's Lord Proprietors, Virginia and North Carolina government officials, and private papers of prominent citizens that revealed many interesting and important facts.

Nana said "Once upon a time in England…" When all of a sudden Adam interrupted her, saying "Blah, blah, blah, Nana I don't mean to be disrespectful and interrupt you but you do remember what that means don't you?

"I like adventures, Nana, but not lectures they're all going to be banished. Okay?"

"Okay," she replied, a little taken aback, then asked, "How do you feel about maps?"

Let's Make An Adventure Map

"Adam one of the great thing that most of the explorers and adventurers did is this, they made maps. Today, we can still see some of the same landmarks and rivers that we see on these old maps that were made hundreds of years ago."

"Look at this 2009 state map of North Carolina," suggested Nana.

"I see New Bern and the Neuse River!" exclaimed Adam.

"Now look on this map made for Raleigh. Can you tell from the landmarks around the Indian village Neusiok where New Bern would be? I said would be Adam, because they made this map 116 years before New Bern was founded, so New Bern wouldn't be on any map, but the land would still be here, right?"

"Right, and the Neuse River is still here," said Adam.

Proud that Adam understood, Nana assured him saying, "Exactly like that Adam, but maybe with a different name.

"Okay," muttered Adam, already comparing the maps. "I've got an idea Nana, let's make our own map for our adventure," suggested Adam. "Then if readers want to they can follow in my footsteps on their own history adventure. We'll write the names that are used today so it will be easier for them if they follow our map."

"Adam I think that is an excellent idea, I just had an idea, too. We could save trees if we make our book available as an e-book that readers can download from the internet."

"Nana, we will still need paper books so we can have book signing parties," advised Adam; bewildered that apparently she had not considered that. Especially since, they had just been talking about going to the New Bern Mall next week to see Nicolas Sparks at his latest book signing party.

"What do you think about this?" Nana asked, changing

the subject, pointing to New Bern on the map with a green highlighter. "You are our navigator and I brought this compass for you to use, let's line up the compass's north with the map's north and go over the route we want to take."

Starting and stopping at New Bern, the highlighter's big florescent green oval stood out on the map. Then Nana began drawing small green circles around each place they wanted to visit, saying: "First, we will go the Union Point Park, leaving New Bern we follow Hwy 70 East to Havelock, where we turn left onto 101 and we will be at the main gate entrance to the Marine Corps Air Station Cherry Point.

"When we leave the base we turn left onto 101, when we reach 306 we turn left, again. From there it's a straight shot to the ferry landing where we catch the Cherry Branch ferry to Minnesott Beach, somewhere around there is where that Pamlico Indian girl probably lived.

"Coming back across the Neuse River we take 306 from the ferry landing back to 101, this time we turn right.

"We'll stay on 101. Just past the base gate is a traffic light where we will turn left to get back onto Hwy 70.

"We follow Hwy 70 to the Crystal Coast Welcome Center, which is just before we get to Morehead City. We can stop there to look at some tourist brochures about the places we want to visit. Leaving the welcome center, we turn left onto Hwy 70, and we stay on 70 all the way to Beaufort.

"In Beaufort we'll stop at the North Carolina Maritime Museum to see the Blackbeard exhibit.

"Then back the way we came on Hwy 70 to Morehead City, where we'll have lunch before we leave the mainland. After lunch, we cross over the Atlantic Beach Bridge to the outer banks, where we turn left onto State Road 58, which runs the length of the island.

"We will be following Carolina's Civil War Trail on 58 to Fort Macon State Park which is located near the end of the island that juts out into the south side of Beaufort Inlet, where Blackbeard wrecked the QAR.

"Leaving Fort Macon, we take 58 to the North Carolina Aquarium at Pine Knoll Shores, where the cutest otters you will ever see live.

"After the aquarium we want to turn right onto 58 towards Indian Beach and we should start looking for somewhere to eat dinner before we leave the outer banks and cross over Bogue Sound, back to the mainland.

"Make sure you look out the windows at the sound when we cross over the bridge Adam. Once you see the incredible colors of the small islands scattered around, you'll understand why they named their town Emerald Isle.

"Then we head for home, keeping on 58 all the way to Maysville where we turn right onto Hwy 17 towards New Bern, which by my calculations is about 128 miles roundtrip.

"Adam, when we stop at the Crystal Coast Welcome Center we can get some brochures about some of the other attractions to visit and then we will plan some other fun things to do. Are you ready for an all day adventure by water?"

"Yes ma'am! I have never been on a ferryboat before, but I have been to the beach and I am very glad we will be on our water adventure for the whole day. I love to swim so much that my mom says I must be 'part frog'."

Pointing to a paragraph on the old map Adam asked, "What does that mean Nana?"

"It explains that this map was copied from maps made by Raleigh's men during their explorations and shows all of the Indian's territories and the location of their towns.

"Compare the maps Adam, you can see that the Neuse River is exactly where is today, but there's a lot of islands near Roanoke Island on Raleigh's map that no longer exist, but Roanoke Island is still there and there is a state park and museum where the colony use to be.

"The explorers said they used the Secotan Indian's name for the Neuse River and on Raleigh's map they show two Neusiok towns. One is near Cherry Point the other one is at Union Point.

"I read about it in a report that is in your boring details section," said Nana with a smile. "It tells that to the Secotan 'ok' meant people and when they joined the name of the Neuse River with the 'ok' it meant that the people of the Neuse River have a town here."

"I guess you could say Adam, that it is because of Raleigh's explorers that the Neusiok tribe became known by the name their enemies gave them; even though that is not the name they gave themselves.

"This book, *The Tuscaroras*, says the Indians who lived here named their river Cau-ta-noh, which means 'Pine-in-Water' and named their tribe Kau-ta-noh, which means 'the people of the 'Submerged Pine Trees'.

"Just think, Adam, 126 years after Raleigh's explorers located that Neusiok Indian town on their map our Baron would buy it and rename it New Bern.

"Adam, Nana can tell you about your Indian ancestors because you're part Indian," interjected Wanda.

"Well, that's news to me! How can I be part Indian mom?" asked Adam, finding it hard to believe. "I'm an American."

"Ask Nana, I want to look at some of these books. This one, *A New Bern Album,* looks interesting. I wonder if it has a picture of the Viking ship at Union Point Park. I use to play on it when I was your age Adam. I wonder what ever happened to it."

"I remember how much fun all the kids had playing on that Viking ship," Nana said, before turning her attention to Adam, saying, "Maybe we can solve that mystery Adam, and I am going to tell you some stories about your Indian ancestors, but not now. I will just say you have Choctaw Indian ancestors on my father's branch of our family tree.

"There is just one more thing Adam, your mom has kindly planned a Christmas Eve surprise adventure into history for us tomorrow afternoon, do you want to go?" asked Nana.

"Yes ma'am!" agreed Adam, eager to continue his adventure into history.

"Adam, maybe we could learn what really was going on around here when the Neusiok Indians, Baron de Graffenried, and John Lawson lived here."

"Please, do not forget the pirates and the Viking ship Nana," pleaded Adam.

Wanda, handing Adam a huge Red Delicious apple added, "And do not forget to take this apple with you tomorrow."

The Second Journey is by a Horse Drawn Carriage, on Christmas Eve

New Bern's First Christmas
The horse's hooves made a lazy, rhythmic sound, clippety-clomping along, pulling the carriage through downtown New Bern on Christmas Eve, 2007.

Adam, Nana, and Nelson, Adam's older brother, waiting beside the sign advertizing the carriage rides, watched the horse and carriage as it traveled up Middle Street to pick them up. Before they setout in the carriage to tour the historic section of New Bern, the driver allowed the horse to eat the apple Adam's mom had given him.

"Who is that?" asked Adam, as the carriage came to a stop, on Pollock Street, between Christ Episcopal Church and City Hall.

"That's Baron Christopher de Graffenried, founder of New Bern, the driver said; you can get out and take pictures."

"Let's take a picture of you and our Baron, Adam. Be careful you don't step on any of the flowers," cautioned Nana.

Nana read aloud from the plaque under the bust: BARON CHRISTOPHER DE GRAFFENRIDE FOUNDER OF NEW BERN, NORTH CAROLINA SEPTEMBER 11,1710 LANDGRAVE OF CAROLINA, BARON OF BERNBURG, LORD OF WORB, WIKARTSWIL AND TRIMSTEIN, GOVERONOR OF YVERTON, KNIGHT OF THE PURPLE RIBBON, MEMBER OF THE ORDER OF SUNSHINE, MASTER OF ARTS, DOCTOR OF LAW, HONORARY CITIZEN OF LONDON.

"Our Baron named New Bern after his hometown of Bern, Switzerland, Adam. Now, here we are almost 300 years latter remembering him as the founder of your hometown."

"That first Christmas Eve in 1710 would have been the very first time Christmas was celebrated in New Bern. At least I think they celebrated Christmas. What do you think Adam?"

"I think they celebrated Christmas, Nana, because Christmas was probably their favorite holiday. It's my favorite, holiday!"

"It's also my favorite holiday!" declared Nana. "But that Christmas Eve was a very long time ago. Maybe we can get a sense of just how long ago 297 years is if we make a comparison. In three years, it will be New Bern's 300th birthday, to make it easy we will round up 297 years to 300 and use your school Christmas vacation for the comparison. Okay?"

"Okay," agreed Adam.

"You have been on Christmas vacation for one week and there are 7 days in a week, so you know how long that has been, right?" asked Nana.

"Correct," answered Adam.

Using the calculator on her cell phone Nana continued, "When we do the math, 7 days multiplied by 300 years equals 2,100 days. 2,100 days divided by the 365 days in a year equals 5.75 years, for easy comparison, we will just say the answer is almost 6 years.

"Now then, Adam, your birthday is soon, you're almost six years old, right?"

"Correct," replied Adam.

"Maybe," suggested Nana, "if you compare your age of almost 6 years to the almost 6 years of Christmas vacation you might get a sense of how long 300 years really is.

"If we started our Christmas vacation on the day you were born we would still be on Christmas vacation."

"You mean it would have been Christmas for my whole life?" asked Adam.

"For your whole life," confirmed Nana.

"300 years is a long time!" exclaimed Adam, somewhat surprised.

Seeming to feel the enormity of a life that was one long Christmas vacation a laughing Adam concluded, "Nana I think we would have so many presents there wouldn't be any room for us and we would have to have another apartment just for presents!"

"That's probably true, but the settlers didn't have that problem Adam. They were far from their hometowns and most of them had a miserable time of it even before they left England. I think they would have wanted to celebrate their traditional Christmas just to cheer everyone up," she replied.

"I think they wanted to cheer up everyone with a Christmas tree so it would make the children happy," concluded Adam. "It made me happy when my mom let us put up our Christmas tree."

"I'm sure you're right, Adam. Some of the settlers brought their families. They came here looking for a better life for their families and certainly wanted their children to be happy.

"The Swiss, German, and English settlers all had a lot of the same traditions at Christmas time. They probably wanted to continue them because, after all, having a Christmas tree to celebrate Christmas started in Germany.

"They started celebrating about four weeks before Christmas by decorating the house with an Advent wreath and waited to decorate the tree on Christmas Eve. You might even have heard that old German song, 'O Tannenbaum', which means in English 'O Christmas tree'.

"We continue the German tradition by having wreaths and an evergreen fir tree but today we have electricity and can use strings of light to light our Christmas trees. Before electricity, they lit the Christmas tree using little candles, setting them on little tin saucers, placed at the ends of the tree's branches so as not to catch the tree on fire, and decorated it with red apples, nuts, dates, pretzels, gingerbread cookies, candy canes, and paper flowers.

"Red roses were the favorite paper flowers because they liked to decorate using red and green colors. We still think of red and green as Christmas colors.

"The first record of Santa was in 1425. The German Santa's name was Saint Nicklaus and he wore a green suite. He wears a red suite in America now because years ago an artist colored his suite red for a Coca-Cola advertisement.

"Even the names of Santa's reindeers Donner and Blitzen are German words meaning thunder and lightening.

"Adam, they decorated the trees to celebrate the birth of Jesus as the light of the world on Christmas Eve by lighting the candles. On Christmas day, the children would get to eat the treats hanging on the tree.

"And their favorite dish for a traditional German Christmas meal, roast goose, could be found here.

"Germans also had a tradition, going back to the year 1329; of making fruit bread they called 'Stollen' by filling the dough with colorful, dried, candied fruits, and several kinds of nuts.

"They consider the Stollen to be the most precious Christmas cake in the world, because they shaped it with tapered ends and a ridge pressed down the center to symbolize the newborn Jesus wrapped in swaddling clothes. I guess you could call it a birthday cake.

"People still have these same traditions at Christmas time, Adam; eating fruitcake and decorating and putting lights on Christmas trees, and having evergreen wreaths, and making gingerbread houses, but I wonder if they know why.

"Germans started the tradition of decorating the Christmas tree with treats. They would make gingerbread cookies shaped like boys and girls, and candy canes to hang on the Christmas tree for decorations and as treats for the children.

"They also burned a Yule Log. Around February, they would cut down a tree and after it had dried for several months, they would soak it in water mixed with fragrant spices. After several more months, waterlogged with the spice they would dry the log out again, so it would be dry enough to burn at Christmas time, filling their homes with the spicy scents of the Yule Log.

"Now, here we are celebrating Christmas in New Bern with a carriage ride."

"I'm glad Mom got us this carriage ride, Nana," admitted

Adam, "I liked feeding the horse an apple even if he did slobber all over it first and I liked the stories about the old days and the near days."

"I'm glad we got to go on this carriage ride, too, and I even liked feeding the horse the rest of the apple that you gave to me when the horse started slobbering all over it. And I'm glad your mom wanted you to see some of New Bern's historical sites, since New Bern is your hometown Adam you should know its history."

"Our Baron only lived in New Bern for two years and nine days, before misfortunes sent him back home again. He left New Bern September 20, 1712 to travel back to England for help, but he only found more misfortunes waiting there. Finally, accepting failure our Baron returned to his hometown, Bern Switzerland, in debt and no one welcomed him home.

"Thinking his life had been a failure he died sad and depressed, sorry he was not able to make New Bern his home.

"That's why I'm glad you want to know the history of your hometown Adam, our Baron, suffered and made many sacrifices trying to do the right thing for New Bern. It's interesting to read some of our Baron's writings, where he tells about what happened to him before and after he came to New Bern.

"Oh, our Baron had high hopes and worked hard for New Bern Adam, and he was proud of New Bern's accomplishments that first Christmas.

"We have to remember his American adventure is not pretend and from the very beginning our Baron had to deal with real treachery, danger, a dozen misfortunes, and calamities, but worst of all Adam he came face-to-face with a rascally gang and was kidnapped by real Indians on the warpath!"

We Have An Easy Life Nowadays

Adam was sitting on the sidewalk curb in front of the bust of Baron Christopher de Graffenried when Nana asked, "Adam can you imagine setting right here at this very spot, say just a few years before any settlers arrived; when it was still the Indian village, Chatooka."

Adam put his elbow on one knee and leaning over cupped his chin in his hand and closed his eyes, imaging.

"Behind some trees or bushes Indian braves would no doubt be watching you, wondering why you are here, and deciding if they wanted to befriend you or kill you or worse, capture you."

Adam jumped up; looking all around just to make sure it was all his vivid imagination, saying with a nervous laugh, "It was definitely scary living here back then."

After they got back into the carriage, Nana continued. "Adam you would not have a cell phone to call 911 and there would be no police or soldiers to save you. Life was full of hardships and danger from wild Indians, wild animals, and especially poisonous snakes.

"I hate to even think of living here during those hot and humid summers before the invention of air conditioning and bug repellent.

"I think night time would have been the worse time because the dark forest was a very dangerous place. It would be so dark that you couldn't see your hand in front of your face and even if you carried a torch you could fall into holes and break bones or fall over the bluffs and drown in the river, and hungry nocturnal animals would be hunting for something to eat.

Nelson said, "Adam, probably, the worse thing for you would be that there were no stores to buy anything, and they didn't have TVs, computers, video games, or Legos® either."

"That's true," said Nana. "There were no grocery stores and people had to trade valuables for food or kill animals and if you weren't careful, some of the animals would eat you first and you had to gather wild fruits, nuts, and try to grow some vegetables to eat or starve. There were no refrigerators or freezers, to keep a supply of food in, so every day was a struggle just to get enough to eat.

"We have an easy life nowadays, compared to then, especially here. Life was so wild back then it's hard for us to imagine the hardships New Bern's first settlers had to endure.

"You wouldn't be sitting on a curb by a paved street. There were no roads or streets, only Indian and animal trails and paths. You would be sitting inside the village of the Neusiok Indians, Adam, surrounded by an immense forest.

"In the beginning when Raleigh's explorers and settlers came to the New World Indians were helpful and friendly. As time went by the Indians became bitter because the settlers tricked, cheated, and abused them, running them off or killing them so they could steal their land, or kidnapping them so they could sell them as slaves.

"It's no wonder then that the settlers referred to the Indians as 'hostiles'."

"Nana, anyone would be hostile if that happened to them."

"You're right Adam, and beside the hostile Indians that first shipload of New Bern settlers had to deal with pirates, too.

"You can read reports about when Lawson and the Palatines first sailed into sight of Virginia and their supply ship was captured by pirates.

"That first shipload of New Bern settlers arrived in the middle of summer and the pirates left them with almost nothing except for their lives so by the time our Baron arrived they were so hot, hungry, depressed, sick, tired, and riled up by mosquitoes and local politicians, they wanted to kill our Baron.

Pointing to the Neuse River on Adam's adventure map, Nana said "Look Adam, we'll see a lot more of history if we follow the adventurers by water."

The Third Journey is by Water, Using Adam's Adventure Maps

Adam's Journey by Water Begins at Union Point Park

The weatherman, Skip Waters, reported New Bern was in the middle of the "dog-days of summer" so it was a perfect day to go on an adventure by water.

As soon as Adam and Nelson got into the car, Nelson reminded Adam to give Nana the $10 bill he was holding in his hand.

Nana asked Adam if he had gotten an allowance.

Looking at Nelson, Adam replied with a wide smile, "No ma'am, my terrific brother Nelson gave it to me so that I could buy an adventure souvenir today."

Just as soon as they dropped Nelson off at Craven Community College, their adventure officially began, so Nana said, "Let's begin at Union Point Park so we can watch the workers dismantling the drawbridge," explained Nana.

"You mean they're tearing down the whole bridge?" Adam asked, shocked at this unexpected news.

"That's right, but they're going to build a new bridge. A lot of things are being done all around New Bern to get ready to celebrate New Bern's 300th birthday next year."

Settling down at the end of the pier, they watched a big red crane lifting huge, brown poles from the water and placing them along the sides of a little blue barge. Just as soon as one little barge was loaded and left another was there to take its place.

"The bridge seems to be coming down fast," observed Nana.

"I just hope they don't scare the fish and ducks," Adam replied.

Nana asked, "Aren't you glad that we can just feed the ducks and not have to kill them for dinner, like the Indians and the settlers had to do?"

"Well, yes! I think that they are way too cute to eat," remarked Adam, pointing out a mallard family swimming past the dock.

"Look at the Neuse River Adam, see how wide it gets? That's the way in and out of the Pamlico Sound, and the way to Roanoke Island, and the way to the Atlantic Ocean, and to the ferry crossing, where we're going next.

"Now, look across the Trent River around where the bridge ends, that's James City.

"Highway 70 crosses that bridge and that's the way to Havelock. When we cross the Trent River, Adam, look to the left and you'll see were we are now at Union Point Park and maybe we could see why our Baron built his cabin here."

"If I was our Baron, Nana, I would've built my cabin where the gazebo is, because you can see up and down both of the rivers," guessed Adam.

"That's as good a guess as any, and it's probably one of the best reasons why our Baron built his cabin here.

"We know it's the perfect spot for a park, but I did see a picture of Bern, Switzerland and I noticed that it's also located in the curve of a river and it looks a lot like this place. So I think that's another reason, you know, because it reminded him of his hometown, but it's time to leave we have a lot of places to visit today."

As they were leaving the pier, Adam discovered a beautiful but very dead dragonfly. He of course kept it for a souvenir.

When they got back to the car, Nana put the dragonfly into a plastic bag so Adam could look at it. Seeing very tiny ants crawling on its eye, Adam said, "Look, Nana, I'm glad you put it in a bag!"

"Yuk! Adam, seeing ants crawling on an eye is creepy, and they are the tiniest ants I have ever seen," said Nana.

Adam decided the bluish-green streak of color on the dragonfly's body was his favorite color, and named it "Dragonfly Blue."

"Remember, Adam, on our way to the ferry, we'll leave New Bern on Highway 70, all the way to Havelock. At Havelock, we turn left onto state road 101 and, just as soon as we turn, we'll be at the front gate to the Cherry Point Marine Air Station. We'll stop there first, because I need to renew my military ID card."

"Pardon Our Noise; It's The Sound Of Freedom"

Just before they got to Havelock Nana asked, "Adam do you see that Ketner Boulevard road sign?"

"I see it, Nana," he replied, as she turned left, onto Ketner Blvd.

After driving a mile or so, Nana parked the car on the right side of the road, saying, "This neighborhood is Ketner Subdivision. That house on the corner is where we lived when your mom was born. I thought this would be a good time to show it to you since we are going to many places today and it'll give you an idea of your region. Plus, our Baron wrote that Mr. Ketner had a very good copy of the map of New Bern and now you know about where his plantation was."

At the base entrance gate, a large welcome sign greeted them with the words, "Pardon our noise, it's the sound of freedom."

"Adam, before we can go through the gates, we have to get a base-pass at the Military Police Station," explained Nana.

Two Military Policemen (MPs) were standing guard at the entrance to Cherry Point Marine Air Station. They both had guns, in holsters strapped around their waists.

When Nana got to the gate, one of the MPs raised his hand gesturing for her to stop, and looked at her ID card and the base-pass. The other MP walked all around the car, looking inside, before letting them go through the gate.

When they parked in front of the RAPIDS office, where they issue ID cards, they saw two marines coming out of the building. Both of them were wearing desert camouflage uniforms.

On the way into the building, Nana commented, "I think God created camouflage so that animals and insects could hide from their enemies. For instance, don't you think your dragonfly's body looks like a twig, its wings resemble leaves, and that streak of Dragonfly Blue, along its body, looks just like a blue sliver of sky?"

Adam agreed, adding, "I think people got the idea to wear camouflage clothes when they saw animals and insects hiding from enemies Nana, and I think those Marines are wearing desert camouflage so they can hide in the desert from their enemies.

Thoughtful for a moment, Adam said, "Maybe the Indians also painted their bodies and faces and wore feathers and furs to be camouflaged in the forest so they could hide from enemies, and hide from animals, too, Nana because I think they probably had to get very close to kill an animal with a bow and arrow."

After Nana got her new ID card and showed Adam the old base hospital where his mom was born she suggested, "Adam, since we're going to ride the ferry next lets stop at the base McDonald's® for a to-go lunch for us to eat on the ferry."

Leaving the base, passing through the gate, Adam noticed, there were no MPs on the exit side of the gate and commented; "Nana, it's a lot easier getting off the base than it is to get on!"

Nana turned left onto 101, before saying, "You're right, Adam, and that's good for us since we don't have to stop, because ferries are on tight schedules it will not wait for us.

"Now, be on the lookout for the 306 road sign, we turn left on 306 to get to the ferry.

Following Our Baron on the Neuse River And Finding a Dragon

About a half-mile from where 306 ended at the Cherry Branch Ferry landing, they saw a long line of cars passing them, going in the opposite direction.

Nana worried aloud, "Adam, I think that long line of cars just got off the ferry."

"I hope there's enough room for us," worried Adam, because now they could see another long line of cars boarding the ferry.

The ferryman guided them onboard and raised the rope gate. As if that was a signal, they immediately could hear and feel the ferry's engines reviving-up and see the ferry was already moving.

"That was close, Adam, but we made it," said Nana. "Ferry

passengers can leave their cars, and walk around the ferry and we can eat our lunch in the passenger's lounge. You bring the bag, and I'll bring the drinks."

Eager to explore, Adam suggested that on the way to the lounge they play Follow-the-Leader; with him, of course, being the leader.

First, Adam led them to the end of the ferry. The ferry's propeller was churning the water, causing a huge wake and splashing sprays of water onto the deck. Dozens of seagulls were flying in a hover over the wake, looking for a lunch of churned up fish.

"Look for fish, too, Nana," encouraged Adam.

Nana replied, "Adam, being this close to birds that are hovering in the air, and seeing them dive into the wake and catching fish is quite an amazing experience, but we're moving very fast. The Neuse River is two miles wide here and it only takes twenty minutes for the ferry to cross so we had better eat lunch. The lounge is upstairs. Do you know the way?"

"Yes ma'am, I'm taking us there, but by a secret path," claimed Adam. Then he suddenly turned right, ducking under the stairs leading to the captain's cabin, coming out on the other side of the ferry.

Windows go all around the captain's cabin and Adam stopped for a moment, before continuing to the stairway leading to the lounge, to watch the captain of the ferry, who was standing at the wheel, maneuvering the ferry through the buoys.

Standing on the second deck, Nana said, "Look Adam, on the other side of Neuse River, a little way up from here is the Marine Corps Air Station Cherry Point, and that's about where the other Neusiok cabin was located that we saw on that old map, and about twenty miles farther up the Neuse River is New Bern.

"Adam, they all came this way. Raleigh's explorers, Lawson, our Baron, the Indians; they all journeyed up and down the Neuse River going right past here, because this was the way to Chatooka.

"Base archeologists have discovered Indian sites on the base, dating back about 10,000 years ago to the Woodland Period. The exact locations of Indians sites located on base are a secret, but you can see pictures of their finds and learn about the sites on the base website.

"On base, near the right side of the old Boy Scout Camp, you can still see a big vein of blue clay in the riverbank. I dug clay from that vein in the summer of 1992, and made ceramic statues and oil lamps and I think the Neusiok built that cabin near the clay to make pottery.

Adam pointed to the far shore, "Look over there, Nana, I can see little sail boats," observed Adam.

"They just look little because they're far away. I think that must be Oriental, because a lot of sailors dock their sailboats there and live on them year-round," she replied.

"Adam, the town of Oriental loves oriental dragons so much they have community events with dragon themes. Every year they have dragon boat races and dragon parades with their giant dragon. Of course, it's not a real dragon, but a giant puppet. It's so long, it takes many people walking underneath it to carry it in the parade through Oriental that they have every New Year's eve, to celebrate the New Year."

Then, seeing a bird sitting on one of the river buoys with a wiggling fish tail dangling from its mouth, Nana, pointing towards the picturesque scene, asked, "Adam do you know what kind of bird that is?"

"Pelican," he relied matter-of-factly, as if he saw that rare sight everyday, then he grabbed her hand saying, "Nana, this way, these stairs lead to my hideout, we can eat there."

Large picture windows lined both sides of the passenger's lounge, creating a pleasant spot for their lunch. Each window had a nice booth and a table. At one end of the lounge, there were newspapers and a big screen TV on a table by the door. There was even a remote control, should a passenger want to change the channel. Best of all, the lounge was air-conditioned.

Sliding into one of the booths, Adam asked, "Do you like my hideout, Nana?"

"I love it!" she replied, "It's the perfect place to eat lunch."

"Nana, let's toast the ferry ride," Adam suggested, raising his cup.

"Okay," Nana agreed.

After that, and before they would take a drink, they would hold out their cups, clink them together, while Adam said, "Three cheers for ferry rides!" or "Hip, hip, hooray for ferries!"

After lunch, Adam led them back to the lower deck to feed the birds. Nana watched Adam and some of the other passengers toss pieces of food into the air, the birds catching some pieces in midair and those they missed floated on the water's surface for only a brief moment before the quickest one swooped down, grasping it in it's beak.

It seemed the food for the birds ran out just as the ferry neared the dock and wanting to be ready to go when the ferry crew lowered the rope gate, everyone hurried back to their cars.

Nana explained, "Adam, to continue our adventure by water, we have to ride the ferry back to the Cherry Point side of the Neuse River."

Once on board the ferry, for the return trip, Adam wanted to explore everything all over again but this time Nana said, "I have a suggestion Adam, this time let's include a little history."

Liking that idea a lot, Adam replied with an enthusiastic,

"Okay! Follow me," Leading her around to the other side of the ferry to some stairs going to the observation deck.

Adam said "This way," but midway up the staircase Adam stopped when he saw some tourists were already there taking pictures. He immediately started backing down the stairs, whispering over his shoulder, "Indians. Go back, Nana! Go back! Hurry or they'll see us."

The stairs ended beside the passenger lounge door. Opening the door Adam whispered, "Let's stay in my hideout until they're gone Nana." Then, sliding into a booth with a view of the stairs he added, "We can keep a lookout from this window."

Nana said, "One thing is certain Adam, when Lawson and our Baron traveled up the Neuse River on their adventure by water it was very dangerous; everything was wild and dangerous back then. We're lucky we don't have to worry about rowing the canoe," causing Adam to laugh at the thought of rowing the ferry.

Nana said, "First Lawson told our Baron that he wanted to go on a canoe trip to find grapes, but our Baron wouldn't agree to such a dangerous trip just to look for grapes since there were plenty of the golden scuppernong grapes growing all around this area.

"After our Baron refused Lawson's first suggestion, Lawson came up with another idea. This time he said they might be able to find a shortcut to Virginia, and maybe harvest some grapes along the way. Lawson probably wanted to harvest the red muscadine grapes he saw on his way to Chatooka to make wine.

"I think he probably wanted to make raisins, too, Nana, because raisins are dried grapes," guessed Adam.

"Good thinking, Adam. The explorers said that the Indians made grape juice to drink and dried grapes to store for later. I guess the settlers wanted to do the same.

"But I have bad news Adam. It's too bad that Lawson didn't accept 'No,' because their canoe trip is doomed. Indians are getting ready to go on the warpath, and Lawson only has a few days left to live.

"The ferry ride isn't long enough to tell you about why the Indians kidnapped our Baron and Lawson. You'll have to read the boring details to find out what happens to them."

Just then, Adam saw the tourists leaving the observation deck and he ordered "Nana, the coast is clear, follow me," then immediately rushed out the door, leading them to the observation deck where there was a huge binocular costing a quarter to look through it for 5 minutes.

Adam was standing on his tiptoes looking through the binocular, when Nana suggested, "Adam turn the binocular so you can look at the shoreline. You never know where an Indian is hiding."

"Nana, the Neuse River is wider here than at New Bern," observed Adam. "But I do see a beach below that hill; do you see it Nana?" he asked, pointing to the left side of the ferry landing.

"Hills with a steep face like that are called bluffs and that's probably the beach at the Bluffs subdivision that's between Camp Seafarer and Minnesott Beach.

"Somewhere over there was the main Indian trading post.

"All of the land you can see on that side of the Neuse River is in Pamlico County, named after the Indians who live there, including the Indian girl in that John White watercolor.

"Look Nana, the ferry is getting close to land," warned Adam."

"It's a good thing you're paying attention," replied Nana. "We better get back into the car so we'll be ready to go."

"Adam, you're the navigator for our water adventure and as soon as you buckle-up, locate us on the map. We want to go back to Havelock, the same way we came.

"Nana I found Havelock!" shouted Adam from the back seat.

"Good, now keep a sharp lookout for Hwy 70 signs Adam, we don't want to get lost."

"Don't worry, Nana, I know, to follow Blackbeard we have to turn left in Havelock."

A Real Pirate Adventure with Cute Otters

"I'm glad we stopped at the tourist center Adam. Before we leave, let's sit in the rocking chairs on the front porch for a few minutes, and look at the map they gave us," suggested Nana.

"I'm glad we stopped and got these brochures Nana," said Adam, selecting the one with a picture of Blackbeard on the front to look at first.

"Adam, on the way to the Maritime Museum I'll tell you some stories about Blackbeard.

"Blackbeard was the most feared pirate in Carolina's history. The sight of Blackbeard was enough to make most of his victims surrender without a fight. Are you ready to see some of the infamous Blackbeard's stuff?"

"Yes ma'am," he replied, getting into the car, "and I'm glad we're going the see Blackbeard first Nana, because I like museums, but what does 'infamous' mean?"

"Infamous means famous for the wrong reasons," answered Nana,

"Researching Blackbeard, I learned he decided to become

a pirate in 1716, when Captain Hornigold told him he would teach him everything he knew about pirating; and the first lesson was for him was to create a fierce reputation and an image for himself to terrify his victims.

"People still create a reputation and an image for themselves; some might wear a suit and tie, another might create a dramatic image like the band KISS. When they are working, the men in the band decorate their faces with white and black face make-up, and wear black outfits decorated with metal spikes, and wear high-heeled/wedge shoes.

"The point Adam is this; the way Blackbeard dressed was more than clothes. Think of it as his work outfit.

"Eye-witnesses say he was tall and his black beard was bushy and braided into pigtails with short colored ribbons and he wore a black three cornered hat and was dressed in a long red coat and black pants and his black boots came to his knees, and, when it came time to fight, he dressed to kill.

"Bandoleers crossed-over his chest, stuffed with knives and pistols attached to the bandoleers with more colored ribbons, and a fine sword on each side of his waist.

"When his victims saw him standing on deck dressed in red and black and with the smoke whirling about his head from the lit slow-burning cannon fuses tucked under the brim of his hat made him look so terrifying that his victims thought the Devil himself, standing in the flames of hell, was robbing them.

"Blackbeard and other pirates were fearless and would capture a ship just coming into harbor in full view of other ships.

"Adam, you've probably seen in pirate movies how pirates would fly false flags on their ship so people wouldn't suspect anything until they were nearby and just before they attacked they raised their pirate flag with a skull and crossbones.

"Officials estimate that Blackbeard plundered more than 50 ships, and I know this will sound unbelievable Adam, but there's no evidence Blackbeard ever had to kill anyone he robbed.

"Blackbeard promised he would ransom the ones who gave up 'peacefully' if not the ones he didn't kill he promised to 'sell as slaves'.

"His threats added to his fierce reputation as the 'blackbeard fury from hell' was enough to cause his victims to surrender without a fight.

"In 1718, England's royal pardon was being offered to all pirates and privateers as long as they swore to give up pirating forever.

"When Blackbeard decided to accept the pardon and settle down in Bath and get married he was in command of 4 ships and over 300 pirates.

"It's told he met his fourteenth wife by chance, a young teenage girl, in Bath. She turned down Blackbeard's proposal of marriage because she was already engaged to be married.

"In order for her to know she was free to marry him, Blackbeard sent her a small bejeweled casket with her fiancées amputated hands inside."

"Ugh! Nana, why would anyone do something so bizarre?"

"It is hard to understand why some people are so cruel, Adam, but it certainly doesn't seem like the best way to start a marriage. The story ends that soon after her marriage to Blackbeard she died from a broken-heart.

"On the way to retirement in Bath, Blackbeard rammed one of his ships, the Queen Anne's Revenge (QAR), onto a sandbar in Beaufort Inlet, near Fort Macon, and ordered forty of his men to transfer the booty to his ship.

"Some say it was an accident, some say it was on purpose.

I believe that Blackbeard was so greedy he planned the wreck so there would be less to share the booty with because when they were finished removing the booty to the other ships Blackbeard sailed away marooning the forty pirates with the wreck.

"We know he sank it there, because that's where treasure-hunters discovered it in 1998. Some of the relics they found at the wreck are on display at the Maritime Museum in Beaufort.

"Adam, Blackbeard's treasure hunters tell about their research in several reports including the one I read on the wwwQARonline.org website, where they tell about how, almost 300 years later, they used the clues that the marooned pirates left behind in English court documents to help them find the QAR.

"It seems that the pirates Blackbeard marooned were rescued by Blackbeard's former partner-in-crime Captain Bonnet.

"In October 1718, Bonnet and his crew were captured and tried for piracy; the London colonial records of the trial record the story the marooned pirates told, which described how Blackbeard sunk their ship and marooned them, and where it happened, and how they came to be with Bonnet."

"You can read all about Blackbeard online and in many books so I will not go into those details for your sake, Adam. I will just say that after sinking the QAR Blackbeard has about 18 weeks to live.

"Blackbeard's pirate friends would come to Bath to visit and it's no surprise that soon Blackbeard was back to pirating with his friends. That is when Blackbeard and hundreds of other pirates made Ocracoke Island their new pirate headquarters.

"England offered a reward of a hundred pounds for Blackbeard, dead or alive, and ordered two ships to find and capture him. Back then, a pound was worth about a $1.66 but back then, a dollar could buy a whole lot more than it will today.

"Lieutenant Maynard was in charge of one of the ships.

"It was a quick battle to the death for Blackbeard, he was tricked by Maynard.

"When Blackbeard fired the first cannon, Maynard knew it would be a fight to the death and he though of a strategy to trick Blackbeard. He ordered some of his men to hide and some to fall and pretend to be dead the next time Blackbeard fired a cannon.

"After the smoke cleared, and seeing the 'dead' men lying on deck, Blackbeard and his men swarmed aboard.

"Just as the pirates crossed over Maynard and all of his men came out of hiding and the dead suddenly came 'alive', catching Blackbeard and his men off guard.

"The fighting was fierce between the hundreds of pirates and the hundreds of soldiers Adam, and it took a lot to kill Blackbeard, he was shot four times and was slashed with a sword twenty times, and one almost severed his head from his body, before the end of the fight.

"The end came when Blackbeard broke Maynard's sword blade in a duel. Maynard threw down his useless sword, grabbed his pistol, and shot Blackbeard in the stomach. Blackbeard said 'Good one lad,' then fell dead at Maynard's feet.

"Maynard finished cutting off Blackbeard's head with Blackbeard's own sword and ordered it hung on the front of his ship as proof Blackbeard was dead.

"I can see the horrible sight in my imagination now, Adam, as Maynard's ship sailed into that Williamsburg, VA harbor with Blackbeard's swollen, severed head dangling from the bowsprit by the hair on the top of Blackbeard's head, the ribbons in his beard fluttering in the wind."

"Nana! Look! I see Blackbeard!" exclaimed Adam, nudging her to look where he was pointing at a life-size cutout of Blackbeard.

"I think you found the Blackbeard exhibit Adam, let's read about the display before we look at the items," suggested Nana, but too late. Adam was already in front of the display, looking at a gun tucked inside the display of items found with the shipwreck.

"I've read about the blunderbuss Nana, and I've seen them in movies, but I never thought I would get to see a real one, and I certainly didn't expect for it to be so big," declared Adam, obviously pleased at the opportunity to see such a rare artifact.

"Not only are you seeing a real blunderbuss but this one belonged to Blackbeard himself since the display says it was recovered form the QAR wreck site."

Not wanting to take his eyes off the incredible array of artifacts, he asked, "What else does it say?"

"It says everything on display in the Blackbeard Exhibit was recovered from the QAR wreckage. Some of the items they cleaned, removing the 300 years of crust covering it, like the blunderbuss you are looking at. But some they left just like they found them, but they can tell what's hidden inside by x-raying it."

Pointing to one of the pictures of the x-rays, Adam said, "Look at this x-ray, Nana. I can tell a cannon ball is inside."

"Adam, besides a little history they won't find much. Don't forget, we know that he emptied the ship before he sailed away so the only things the treasure-hunters will find is stuff Blackbeard forgot to take, didn't want, or accidently left behind.

"Oh! Adam, listen to this! It says they did find some Spanish gold coins and replicas are for sale at the museum gift shop."

"Nana, I want to see the replicas, don't you? I'm glad Nelson gave me money to buy a souvenir because I might want to buy one of the coins if I have enough money."

"Okay." Nana said. "After we visit the museum shop Adam, we'll leave the mainland and crossover to one of the islands and explore Fort Macon. A lot of interesting and important things happened along Carolina's outer banks."

"Don't Fall Into The Fort!"

"Nana, on the map it looks like 58 ends at Fort Macon so after we go over the bridge turn left and keep driving until you get there."

Parking the car in the lot beside the fort Nana confirmed, "You're right, Adam, 58 really does end here because we've reached the end of the island that juts out into Beaufort Inlet and over there is the Atlantic Ocean.

"Adam before we go into the fort, let's take your picture with that Civil War Trail sign and that warning sign."

"Oh my God Adam, stop walking, it looks like you're about to fall into the fort!"

Once off the knoll overlooking the fort, Adam said, "I was just curious, Nana I want to see if I could see Beaufort Inlet. I didn't know the fort was dug into the ground."

"The North Carolina Museum of History's website says Blackbeard's QAR was found in shallow water at the south end of Beaufort Inlet close to Fort Macon, so if they are diving for artifacts today maybe we can see their ship from the other end of the fort.

"Reports say there are signs that someone tried to free the QAR from the sandbar, but I don't think it was Blackbeard.

"Adam I think this is what happened. Blackbeard had the forty pirates unload the QAR onto the other ships and after they finished Blackbeard left without them. The forty pirates couldn't stay on the sinking ship so when they realized Blackbeard was sailing away without them you know they were scrambling to save themselves from drowning.

"I think the marooned pirates at first tried to refloat the QAR in an effort to save themselves but when they couldn't free the ship, the rising tide forced them to save themselves, and this island is the closest land to the wreck," Nana said, pointing to the island on Adam's adventure map. Now you can see why I believe Blackbeard's marooned crew came to this end of the island."

"Nana there must have been Indians here because at the other end of the island there's a town named Indian Beach."

"When Raleigh's men came here there were Indians all along the coastal islands. A lot of history occurred along Carolina's outer banks, Adam. In fact, Raleigh's explorers tell about how their ships were in constant danger of shipwreck, on the shoals around the outer banks. That area along the outer banks from Cape Lookout to Hatteras Island is 'Raleigh Bay' on our NC map.

"Over the years since then, thousands of ships have shipwrecked up and down the outer banks and now the area is known as the 'Graveyard of the Atlantic' and there's a Graveyard of the Atlantic Museum in Hatteras, NC.

"At lot of other important things happened along the outer banks, too. For instance, in the 1840's Fort Macon was captured a couple of times during the Civil War.

"About a hundred years later, during World War II, in the first seven months of 1942, German submarines and U-boats sunk almost 400 of our ships, and they estimate that 5,000 people onboard died, that's when they started calling the area around Cape Lookout 'Torpedo Alley'.

"Because Germans were lurking off the Atlantic coastline of America a shore-side blackout of city lights was ordered to keep American ship's silhouette from being seen against the horizon and attacked by the enemy.

"Adam, entire American coastal cities cut off streetlights and fixed stop lights with slats so that only dim slivers of light would shine down. People who lived along the coast painted their windows black or tarred them or hung blackout curtains over the windows in their houses and businesses so that when they did have lights on you could not see even a sliver of light from outside.

"There's a display at Glenburnie Park that Dylan Simel created for his Eagle Scout Project; where he tells the story about when it was called Camp Battle and 383German prisoners-of-war were kept there.

"During the day they would take the prisoners to work, some worked in potato fields in Pamlico County, some worked at sawmills in New Bern, or other places.

"Because his family has lived here for many generations, New Bern is also Oscar Kafer's hometown and I asked him if he would tell me a couple of stories about something that had happened to him around here when he was about your age and that I could tell you about for your adventure into history.

"He said I could tell you this: When he was 7 or 8 years old a sawmill use to be about where the Comfort Inn is now, beside Union Point Park, and he would go there and try to talk to the German prisoners.

"Mr. Kafer said that he knew how to speak a little German because his grandmother and some of his other German relatives who spoke German. In fact, one of his uncles emigrated here from Germany and opened a bakery downtown on Middle Street where the Cow Café is now in the Kafer Building. You can still see his family's name on the side of the building.

"He also told me a funny story about something scary that happened to him one night during World War II.

"One summer, Mr. Kafer and about 9 other boys were staying in a cabin on Harkers Island and occasionally, at night, when American ships and German U-boats and subs had a firefight around Cape Lookout, they could see flashes of light from the explosions, and the flames and the smoke rising from the burning ships until they sank.

"Of course, Harkers Island was on black-out, too, and he remembered the blackout curtains covering the windows of their cabin, and in the center of the ceiling there was a bare light bulb with a long string hanging from it, which turned the cabin light on and off.

"Well, one night, at bedtime, Mr. Kafer and his friends were horse-playing in the cabin. They were entertaining themselves by trying to scare one another. Jumping from bed-to-bed while trying to catch the string that hung from the ceiling light and pulling on it so the light would go out, leaving them in pitch darkness.

"They were so rambunctious that when they jumped, from one bed to another, the beds would hit the blackout curtains. The Home Guard soldiers on patrol, to guard against Nazi spies coming ashore, saw several quick flashes of light the wiggling curtains let escape.

"All of a sudden, a lot of soldiers bashed in the door to the cabin, busting into the room with their bayonets mounted on the ends of rifles pointed at the boys. You can just imagine what reaction the boys had."

"Yea, Nana, I imagine they were more scared of the bayonets than of the dark."

"I imagine you would be correct, Adam.

"Well, at first the soldiers thought spies had been flashing messages to the German subs and after they bashed in the door, they herded them all outside and searched their cabin."

"What did Mr. Kafer do, Nana?" wondered Adam out-loud.

"Mr. Kafer said he didn't remember doing anything, that he was probably to scared, but what he did remember was that some of the boys were crying and very upset and a couple were probably so scared they were hysterical.

"After the soldiers learned they had just been horse-playing, and that they were not spies or up to any mischief, they tried to calm the boys down. To calm them down, Mr. Kafer said that the soldiers started joking around with them and even gave them some whisky to drink.

"The war had an unusual effect on New Bern because two-thirds of the settles who made it here when New Bern was founded were German, but during World War II Germany was the enemy of the United States and New Bern focused more on the fact that it was a Swiss colony.

"That also reminds me of something that Mr. Jerry Stapleford once told me. He had traveled around the world eight times in ten years when he worked for the Army, inspecting military dining facilities for all of the branches of the military. He said that feeding the troops was so important that there was a famous army adage about it 'An army doesn't march on their feet, they march on their stomach.' Which reminded me about the main problem our Baron had, feeding so many people, and how he could have had a better chance at success if he had had Stapleford helping him.

"It's only been in recent years that we celebrate New

Bern's German settlers, again. Now, every year we celebrate the German festival, Oktoberfest, at the Farmer's Market. Let's plan to go to the Farmers Market during Oktoberfest this year," suggested Nana.

"Okay," he replied. "And Nana, you can see the water from the Farmer's Market, so let's pretend we're on the lookout for German submarines."

"Okay," she answered "but that all happened in the 1940's. Right now, when we go through the fort's entrance gate we'll be in the 1840s."

Crossing over the bridge to the fort's entrance, they noticed, on the right, a park ranger standing near a stack of cannon balls, telling stories about the fort to a group of children sitting on the stairs, so they went the other way.

After going through the rooms and looking at artifacts Adam suggested, "Let's climb these stairs Nana, maybe we'll see the Blackbeard's treasure hunter's ship."

"Okay but I do want to remind you that I get vertigo when I look down from high places," warned Nana when they reached the top of the stairs.

"Especially if I get close to the edge so don't expect me to come any closer than this cannon," Nana added while wrapping one arm around the cannon's barrel.

"But I do want to take some pictures of you, but we can't stay long, I'm already worried about how I am going to get down. I can't believe you got me up here!" declared Nana, taking several photographs of Adam, peering over the top of the fort, looking for the treasure hunters.

"I don't know what your mother's going to say when she sees these pictures," moaned Nana. "Please, come down Adam, this adventure is getting to adventurous for me let's go to the aquarium," pleaded Nana, "Now!"

"Why Is It So Dark In Here?"

"Can you see yet?"

"No," Adam replied. "Can you?"

"I can see a little better now that my eyes are getting use to it," Nana answered.

"Nana, because the fish tanks are lit up I think they turned out the lights so you can see the fish better."

"But it's really dark in here and we have to stay together every second, I mean within touching distance 'together', okay?" she asked.

"Okay," promised Adam.

"Look at the sharks Nana, I think that one is stuck between those rocks," staying to watch until it finally wiggled through and swam away.

After the grand tour of the aquarium, they began wondering where the otters were. Seeing a large group in front of a display Adam suggested they check out what everyone was looking at.

"Of course such cute otters would draw a crowd," admitted Nana.

"Let's sit on the bench and watch them for a while Nana," suggested Adam.

After being entertained by their antics for several more minutes Adam confided, "Nana, it's a good thing we didn't come here first because I could watch these otters play all day."

"Me, too," said Nana. "Let's come back soon for an otter-day adventure, but today we have a lot of other things to do. You should know what real live poisonous snakes that live around here look like. They were some of the Indians worst enemies and they have a snake exhibit. To get there we have to follow this nature trail.

"We'll walk the trial fast Adam, it'll be good exercise, but we also want to hurry because we have one last thing to do on you water adventure, bumper boats."

"I love bumper boats Nana but let's eat pizza at the arcade first. I'm hungry and seeing all of this water makes me thirsty."

On the way home Nana said, "Life is a lot different around the outer banks now, than it was during the Civil War, but the Civil War Trail does not end here Adam, we can follow it to James City.

The Forth Journey is by Land, Following the Civil War Trail

The Founding Of James City

"Adam, I want to tell you some true stories about slavery, some things that happened around here during the Civil War, and about the founding of James City.

"In 1862, during the Civil War, Union forces captured New Bern, and New Bern became Union Headquarters for Eastern North Carolina.

"Union soldiers stationed here would go far into the countryside on raids, all around New Bern, and they rescued thousands of slaves, bringing them back to New Bern and freedom.

"A slave's life was cruel and hard. It was cruel because they lost their freedom. Their owners could rent and sell them and a slave's child would be born enslaved, and it was against the law for anyone to help slaves escape slavery.

"Their lives were hard because they had no choices. Owners could force them to work at whatever job they wanted them to do and they could not choose what they ate, what clothes they wore, or even where they slept.

"Adam, look at this advertisement," said Nana, "it's dated December 20, 1774. It was a news announcment published by a New Bern businessman. He wanted to let people know his ship was 'Coming from Africa with a parcel of healthy slaves consisting of men, women and children…'and he wanted to let everyone know he was selling them from his store at Union Point '…for cash or farm produce'."

"Union Point?" questioned Adam surprised slaves had been sold at his favorite park.

"Yes, Union Point. I was also surprised," Nana confessed.

"You mean he actually sold little children?" asked Adam, hardly able to believe such a thing could have happened in his hometown.

"It's hard to understand how a New Bern businessman like Edward Batchelor could send his ship to Africa to kidnap children so he could sell them into slavery for a bushel or two of corn at Christmas time but it was really more horrible than that." Nana replied.

"Children might be sold to one owner and mothers might be bought by a different owner and fathers dragged off by another owner, to only God know where," murmured Nana, conjuring up those dreadful scenes that had actually taken place in Adam's hometown.

"A lot of comments have been written about what Lawson and our Baron wrote about slaves but not many about what our Baron's partner, Franz Michel wrote," she said.

"Michel wrote that there were large numbers of slaves for sale; from young children to old men and women, mostly brought here from Guinea and Jamaica, and they arrived entirely naked, except for a few who had colored coral necklaces around their necks and arms.

"That groups of slaves would be brought out chained together and he points out how you could pick the ones you wanted to buy. He even wrote that they usually cost from 18-30 pounds each; then Michel compares the cost of buying a slave with a horse costing 3-8 pounds each.

"Adam, in 1700 a pound was worth about $1.66 making a slave cost from $30 to $50 and you could by a horse from $5 to $13.30.

"Michel wrote that slaves were cheap to keep because each day they only received a meager serving of ground maize that they boiled with water to eat, calling it 'hominy'. Sometimes they would mix it with water and fry it into a cornbread, and they would try to catch turtles and anything else they could find to eat.

"Michel said he tasted slave food once and that the hominy was okay but he could hardly eat their bread.

"I hope these stories will help us understand how slaves must have felt during the Civil War when Union Soldiers rescued them, Adam."

"I know it will, Nana, because now I know more about slavery, and I definitely would not want to be a slave, even if my master was nice; and I do not believe anyone should be kidnapped or made a slave."

Nana said, "That's how most people feel now Adam, but buying slaves was the first thing our Baron, Lawson, Michel, Pollock, Moseley, and most of the rest of the settlers who could afford it did, just as soon as they got here. I said just as soon as they got here because in Europe slavery was illegal.

"When the Civil War started, on April 12, 1861 North Carolina had 300,000 slaves owned by 40,000 families. Most families owned one or two but some, like Pollock and Moseley, owned hundreds to work in the fields on their plantations.

"Some Union soldiers wrote about what happened on March 14, 1862 when they captured New Bern.

"One soldier told about when his regimen landed at a New Bern wharf on Trent River.

"He said a crowd of New Bern slaves had gathered on the wharf to greet them, dancing all around the wharf, singing, and waving white scraps of cloth.

"Adam, I saw this picture of two young slave boys in the Sun Journal newspaper today," said Nana, holding up the picture, so he could see them.

"One looks to be about your age. The other boy looks to be about five years old. It appears as if someone sat them on top of this big barrel because the barrel is too tall for either to have climbed to the top by themselves."

"They don't look very happy," observed Adam.

"The story says the photo was taken by a famous Civil War photographer and it was found in the attic of an old house in North Carolina."

"Nana, maybe the kids had just been rescued by the soldiers and the photographer put them on top of the barrel to take their picture," guessed Adam.

"You maybe correct, Adam," agreed Nana. "Since it's one of his Civil War pictures maybe he did take it in New Bern.

"The soldiers probably had their hands full trying to set up tents and caring for the children," Nana said, "because of the way slave families were split-apart many of the children were orphans.

"Adam, 'Freedmen' was the name used by the government for all freed slaves; men women, children, or Indians,"

"Indians!" exclaimed Adam.

"Yes," Nana answered. "I've even seen the names of some of our Choctaw ancestors on the Choctaw Freemen Rolls.

"Chaplin Horace James was in charge of the Freedmen in New Bern and it was his job to set up the new government programs created to help the Freemen start new lives. If the boys in the picture came here, Chaplin James would have taken care of them.

"The founding of James City began as a camp set up in order to help the thousands of New Bern refuges begin their lives of freedom," said Nana.

"In the spring of 1863, James City was settled on about 30 acres of land that had once belonged to Governor Richard Dobbs Speight. The January 1864 census shows that 2,798 Freedmen were living in James City.

"The settlement was known first as the Trent River Camp but the residents renamed it James City because they wanted to show their appreciation for Chaplin James helping them begin their new lives as Freedmen.

"Adam, I think those first residents of James City and those Union soldiers who rescued them would be proud to know that one hundred and forty eight years later Barack Obama, an African American man whose mother was a white American and whose father was a black African, would become the 44th president of the United States.

The Fifth Journey is by Car, Hearing Stories about the Near Times

Real Witches

Adam almost chocked on his tea when Nana said she personally knew some 'real witches' who once lived in New Bern. Between coughs, Adam studied her face to see if she was joking. As soon as he caught his breath he asked, "Are you sure they were real witches Nana?"

"Adam, not only were they real witches, Gavin, Yvonne, and Bronwyn Frost are still witches since they are all alive and blog about witchcraft on the internet.

"The Frosts lived in North Carolina for about 20 years, which makes me believe that New Bern will become a tourist attraction for people interested in the history of the Church and School of Wicca and witchcraft.

"What do you think about this idea, on our drive to Vanceboro's Strawberry Festival I'll tell you some true stories you might find interesting, and then we can include the stories in our book.

"Would you like to hear about how Vanceboro Farm Life Elementary School got its name? What happened to the lost Viking ship? What happened when your mother spent the night at the witch's house, when she was about your age? And what happened to Uncle Joel when he was seven and the High Priest of the Church and School of Wicca hit him in the mouth with his fist?"

"Well, yes!" exclaimed Adam in an exasperated voice tone requiring an exclamation point; because his face seemed to say, "What a ridiculous question, anyone would want to hear those stories."

Just as soon as they turned right onto Hwy 43, heading towards Vanceboro Nana began, saying, "It was towards the end of the 1970's when the witches moved to New Bern.

"Gavin and Yvonne Frost were coming from the post office when they stopped at my real estate office to inquire about a house for sale on East Front Street, around where Dr. Hand III has his dental office now.

"It was a strange meeting. Right after our greetings and introductions, Gavin opened the mailbag he had been carrying. Holding the bag in the air chest-high, he suddenly turned the bag upside down dumping a huge pile of envelopes onto my desk.

"As the envelopes started falling onto the desk Gavin instructed, 'Select one of the envelopes, any one it doesn't matter which one'.

"Sticking my hand into the center of the pile I pulled out a blue envelope and handed it to Gavin.

"Opening the envelope, Gavin turned it over so that a check and a clipped form, from one of their advertisements for new students who wanted to learn witchcraft, fell out onto the pile of envelopes, saying 'Checks are in all of them'.

"Gavin explained that they were moving to New Bern; and they were the founders of the Church and School of Wicca.

"Adam, in the olden days Wicca meant a practicing witch or in other words the practice of sorcery. You might even say the name of their church literally means the Church and School of Sorcery, or the Church and School of Witchcraft," explained Nana.

"Like Hogwarts, in Harry Potter?" Adam asked, having recently read several Harry Potter books.

"Not really, students didn't live at the witches' house like Harry lived at Hogwarts, and there has never been any report of witches flying around on broom sticks around here, at least not that I know of.

"But that day, Gavin went on to tell us they founded the Church and School of Wicca in 1968, and he was the Church's Archbishop and High Priest, and his wife the High Priestess.

"Gavin proudly proclaimed they could prove they were real

witches because in 1972 the United States Internal Revenue Service (IRS) recognized their form of witchcraft as a religion.

"They said they were able to create the Church and School of Wicca because of their superior intelligence. Claiming, he held doctorates in Physics and Mathematics, and Yvonne was a certified genius and a member of Mensa; pointing out that only the top two percent of the general population in the whole world was intelligent enough for Mensa to invite them to join.

"That all of the envelopes contained money because people were responding to ads they had placed, mainly in comic books, to learn witchcraft by mail. That was how their church school started out and made money to pay for all of their needs, living expenses, and to buy houses.

"They had a daughter, Bronwyn, who was your mom's age. Since she was new in town, and we lived nearby, I introduced her to Wanda.

"Before long Bronwyn spent the night at our house then wanted Wanda to spend the night at the house they bought on East Front Street.

"Wanda's sisters and brothers teased her about what might happen if she really spent the night with witches.

"Trying to scare her with warnings to be very careful because the witches might try to cast a spell over her if she went to sleep and, if they succeeded, she would never wakeup until a prince or a frog kissed her.

"Telling her that most witches wanted a cat but not just any cat, they wanted a 'magic-cat'. That meant they needed real children that they could turn into a 'magic-cat' by tricking them into eating a magic-potion. Once the children ate the magic-potion, the witches could turn the children into a cat whenever the children heard them say the magic-words, 'Kitty Cat'.

"After I assured her that her sisters were just trying to scare her, that our prayers would protect her, and that I would pick her up if she got scared, no matter what time it was, your mom bravely spent the night at the witch's house.

"The next morning I asked her about the sleepover and wondered what she ate for dinner and breakfast and if she had been scared.

"She said that she had fun playing with Bronwyn but that she was scared a little bit when it was time to eat. That she was very surprised and suspicious when they had raw soup for dinner and breakfast. I asked her to describe the soups.

"For dinner, Wanda told how they each had a soup bowl filled with 'bits and pieces of raw vegetables, like carrots, peas, potatoes and celery', in some kind of 'bloody-red looking soup', although she did admit it was probably just tomato juice and that they had some sort of curious, green tea to drink.

"She explained, that since she had been leery of the strange soup she told the witches she wasn't hungry and she only pretended to sip the tea, just to be safe incase they had slipped a magic-potion in it.

"For breakfast, Bronwyn told her they were having 'fruity-soup'. She said she could smell pineapple and thought the cloudy soup was pineapple juice in their bowls with bits and pieces of fruit in it, but she didn't eat any 'fruity-soup' either because she wasn't able to guess what kind of fruit was in the soup."

"Nana, I think it's better to be safe and hungry, than full and sorry," said Adam.

"You're right," Nana replied. "Your mom explained to me that she thought the witches ate raw food because witches cook their potions for magic-spells, so if they didn't eat anything cooked no one would be able to slip magic-potions into their food.

"The story is also interesting Adam because it inspired your cousin, Sean Ludden, to nick-name your mom, 'Aunt Kitty Cat'.

"Sean was about four years old when he heard the story. Someone suggested to Sean that he might be able to see Aunt Wanda change into a kitty cat if he said the 'magic-words' loud enough for her to hear them. From then on, whenever Sean saw Wanda he would chase her, yelling, 'Aunt Kitty Cat'.

"One of Wanda's sisters, your Aunt Jackie, had a cat with a litter of kittens a couple of weeks old and one day they decided to play a trick on Sean.

"When Sean saw Wanda he of course started chasing her yelling 'Aunt Kitty Cat'. This time Wanda ran into Jackie's bedroom slammed the door closed and hid. Jackie was in the room waiting and when Wanda closed the door Jackie placed one of the kittens on the floor in the middle of the room then she hid.

"When Sean finally got the door open, he only saw the kitten sitting on the floor in middle of the room. Convince he had transformed Wanda into a kitten, by saying the magic-words, Sean picked the kitten up and carried it all through the house, telling everyone how he had turned Aunt Wanda into 'Aunt Kitty Cat'.

"But back to the story about real witches. Adam all of the time I knew the witches, when they lived in New Bern, they worked from their home teaching witchcraft. In the beginning they did all of the writing for their sorcery lessons, magic spells, rituals and newsletters and printed them using an old hand-cranked mimeograph machine.

"First, they lived on East Front Street, then they moved to Metcalf Street, just across from the garden gate in back of the Governor's Palace, then they moved near the old train station, sometime after that they moved to Pamlico County, now they live in West Virginia.

"The witches were living on Metcalf Street, across from Tryon Palace's garden gate, when Gavin hit Uncle Joel in the mouth.

"We lived in the big house on the corner of Broad and Metcalf Streets; you remember where I took your picture sitting on the front steps the other day."

"Yes, I remember, but you didn't say anything about witches living around there," accused Adam.

Nana apologized, "I'm sorry, I wasn't trying to hold anything back.

Seeing the scow still on Adam's face Nana explained, "Remember, it was the 4th of July and we had to hurry so that we would be at the Governor's Palace in time to hear the reading of the Constitution and watch the Fife and Drum Corps perform. It didn't seem to be the right time to tell you stories about witches.

"Back then our house was only about a block and a half from the witch's house and one afternoon Joel was near the witch's house when something happened.

"All I know for certain is Gavin grabbed Joel by the neck of his t-shirt and started shaking him back and forth, and so hard that Gavin's fist would collide with Joel's mouth and cheek. Each blow of Gavin's fist slammed Joel's mouth against his teeth, cutting the inside of his mouth and loosening several of his baby teeth.

"I was still at work, but two of your mom's teenage sisters, Aunt Starr and Aunt 'Goddess' Donna, were at home when

Joel came in crying and just as soon as they saw blood all over Joel's mouth and t-shirt, Aunt 'Goddess' called the police.

"I don't know what Gavin told the police when they arrested him I just know it's serious when you hurt anyone, especially when an adult hurts a seven year old child.

"I had to go to the police station and talk to the District Attorney about pressing charges against Gavin for assault and I did.

"The next day a friend suggested I should reconsider and allow a Dismissal without Prejudice, meaning that should Gavin do anything else he could be re-charged for the original assault.

"Joel was only seven and I though she had given me good advice because I knew that Joel would be frightened when he saw that the witch who had hit him was sitting in the courtroom looking at him when he testified.

"I wanted Joel to feel safe and explained to him about the Dismissal and that he didn't have to worry about Gavin hurting him again, so that's how it ended.

"During those years, I learned some unusual things about the Church and School of Wicca. One of the most surprising, at least to me, is the fact that they do not necessarily get married for life. Gavin and Yvonne said they only married for seven years at a time.

"I was curious to learn if you could really get married for only seven years and asked my attorney. He explained that he had never heard of a seven-year marriage before but a marriage was a contract between two people and it would be like any other contract and could be for seven years or for as long as they wanted the contract to last.

"Adam that means that when the time on the marriage contract was up you would no longer be married because the contract had ended and you would not have to get a divorce.

"He said the only reason someone has to get a divorce to end their marriage contract is because when they got married they said it was for life and to end that marriage contract one of them would have to get a divorce or die."

A Viking Ship And A Viking Trait

"Adam, from that day at your house, when your mom asked us to find out what happened to the Viking ship I began asking people if they remembered it, most did but they also wondered what happened to it.

"I asked Dr. Hand if he knew anything about the Viking ship because he and his wife are both well known in New Bern for their love of local history. He said he thought they built the Viking ship to be in Eric cigarette advertisements and after they were finished with the ads, they gave the ship to New Bern, but around the time that he went to dental college he thought New Bern loaned it to a movie studio for a Viking movie.

"With this information, I went to the library and talked to Mr. John B. Green III, because he knows a lot about New Bern's history, or knows where you can find the information. He suggested sending an email to Mr. Victor Jones Jr., Department Head of the library's Kellenberger Room / Special Collections.

"My email explained we were curious about the Viking ship and asked if he could help us answer four questions.

Why was there a Viking ship at Union Point Park?

Who built it?

What happened to it?

What was the name of the movie?

"Adam I was so surprised when I received his answer

because Mr. Jones solved the Viking ship mystery in just a few hours. He not only answered the questions but he also included other interesting facts.

"It turns out that Dr. Hand was correct. Commodore Boat Works (CBW) built New Bern's Viking long ship, Erik II, in 1965 for the P. Lorillard Company.

"Adam, Lorillard is America's oldest tobacco company and the boat was built to use in their Erik cigarette ads and commercials, it was named Eric II because the company had used another Viking long ship named Eric in earlier cigarette ads.

"Once Lorillard finished making the Eric II commercials it was refurbished and given to the city of New Bern because CBW had built the ship here, it was placed in Union Point Park and dedicated by the city in April 1974.

"In 1977-78 it was again refurbished and used in a movie, *The Norsemen*. After the movie, the Viking ship returned to Union Point Park where it eventually 'deteriorated beyond repair' and demolished by the city; 'before someone got hurt' according to the Sun Journal newspaper article Mr. Jones read.

"Mr. Jones also added, that the newspaper article said the Chamber of Commerce kept two of the shields that lined the sides of the boat. However, he was not sure if they still had the shields.

"Adam, can you believe it, the Viking ship mystery is solved?"

"Nana, do not tell mom Mr. Jones solved the mystery, she can find out what happened to the Viking ship when she reads our book," suggested Adam, with a mischievous grin lighting up his face.

"Okay," Nana agreed, smiling. "I am glad that you want to surprise your mom."

"Nana, I am glad Mr. Jones solved the Viking ship mystery because I'm part Viking. Did you know that?"

"Yes, I do remember your Aunt Starr telling us that your mother's curved little fingers is a Viking trait. I think Vikings developed that trait because their long ship had only a small sail and they still had to row it.

"I was surprised and curious, when Starr told us about the Viking trait, and I researched Vikings on the internet.

"History stories tell about how, around a thousand years ago, Vikings settled Ireland and gave Ireland its name; settled in Scotland and named an area there; then settled in France, where they were called Normans, meaning they had come from the north, and their settlement there is still called Normandy.

"Viking's Duke of Normandy waged a war killing England's king and he became England's King William the Conqueror in 1066, when he was 39 years old.

"It seems that even after many years genes can still pass on traits, since both you and your mother definitely have inherited that Viking trait.

"We are almost to Vanceboro so I better tell you about when your school was a farm.

Your School Was Really a Farm

"I bought an old book, *Young People's History Of North Carolina*, because it was a schoolbook used in 1924. It explains that North Carolina started farm life schools so new discoveries in science could become useful to farmers and help them increase the yields of their crops and animals and earn more money, and how to operate a farm efficiently so they could save money.

"Farmers wanted their children to learn the art of farming

using the latest science and to train them for farm life. The North Carolina General Assembly passed the County Farm Life School Act in 1911 that would establish 19 schools to teach agriculture in North Carolina.

"In November, 1913 the Craven County Farm Life School in Vanceboro was the first Farm Life School to open.

"There were 35 students, 12 boys and 23 girls, enrolled the first-year. In the second year, there were 12 new students, 7 boys, and 5 girls."

"Nana, do you mean there were only 35 students for all of the grades?"

"I'm not sure how it worked Adam, but only 35 students attended school that first year. They probably had more animals on the farm than children in school. In the beginning, it was Vanceboro Farm Life School and I think it started out as a high school, later it became Vanceboro Farm Life Elementary School.

"On the internet you can see pictures of some the students who went to your school back then. The girls are all dressed the same in long white dresses and wearing white aprons and caps. Some of the boys wore suits and some were dressed in overalls.

"The school had its own farmland to grow crops, barns for animals, workrooms, domestic science rooms, and kitchens.

"So that they could live on the 90 acre campus, there was a house for the principle of the school, a cottage for the farmers, and a dormitory for students.

"There was also a power plant. The records show the new buildings and equipment cost about $25,000. It would cost millions of dollars to build it today.

"The school also had a small herd of cows and some pure-breed hogs. They used the animals both to educate the students and as food for the school. Online, you can find records of those pure-breed hogs, see their pictures, and their names.

"Farm Life Schools not only gave boys the opportunity to study the science of farming and taking care of farm machinery and animals, Adam, but the school also gave girls the opportunity to study farm life home economics; and other homemaking skills like sewing, canning, preserving and cooking the food they grew on the farm.

"What do you think about the history of your school Adam?"

"Well, I wish we still had animals at school, but I wouldn't want to spend the night," he replied.

"I can understand that," Nana said, "but in 1913 there were no school busses and kids walked, sometimes miles, to get to school. Craven County is big and some kids lived to far away to walk to school. If there had not been a place at school for them to live, a lot of them probably would not have been able to go to Vanceboro Farm Life School. Plus they had to take care of the animals so it made sense to live there."

"Nana, I'm sorry to interrupt but I can see the Strawberry Festival parade."

"We got here just in time. I think later it will be sunny and hot maybe you should buy a hat and sunglass after the parade. We can buy some homemade strawberry ice cream and while we are eating it, we can walk around and check out the rides and booths, and make plans.

Adam stopped and pointed towards a little trailer with a table in front of it that had a sign saying 'Tickets for Sale'. "Look, Nana there is no line yet at the ticket table, I think there is going to be long lines to get on these terrific rides maybe we should buy tickets for the rides first."

Soon Nana was taking pictures of Adam; on the giant

yellow slide, on the 'Fun Tubs' with several school friends, and on the swings ride with Mrs. Wooten's grandchildren.

By mid-morning, there was already a huge crowd, and they were glad they had arrived early. After eating nachos with cheese, barbequed chicken, and homemade ice cream, they bought eight pints of strawberries to take home.

As they were driving away Nana remarked, "I wonder if the students planted strawberries on Vanceboro's Farm Life School's farm in 1913. What do you think?"

Adam replied, "I think they probably did Nana but I wonder if the Indians had strawberry festivals."

"Maybe," said Nana. "We know the Indians had corn festivals, but did you know Indians named the months after its main food, March was 'Strawberry Time'.

"There are some other things we know for certain Adam; before the good times came there were the killing times."

The Sixth Journey is by Research, Following Paper Trails for Hundreds of Years

Why and How Our Baron Became a Carolina Landgrave

"Adam, weather often plays an important part in history and it probably did when our Baron decided to move here. The records say that in 1709 the weather was coming to the end of a 100-year ice age across Europe, where our Baron, the Swiss, and the Palatines lived," explained Nana.

"October 1708 began a bitterly cold winter that was the coldest in a hundred years. It started snowing on January 25, 1709, and did not stop until February 6. It was so cold dead birds fell out of the sky, frozen to death while they were flying.

Shocked at the news, Adam exclaimed, "Nana, if frozen birds were falling out of the sky I would want to move too!"

"So would I," agreed Nana. "And with dead birds falling out of the sky and a snow storm lasting almost two weeks it is no wonder that so many people wanted to move to Carolina because of books like Lawson's. In his book, *A New Voyage to Carolina,* Lawson calls Carolina a 'summer-land'.

"This is also about the time when a couple of our Baron's future partners, Franz Ludwig Michel, Esquire, and George Ritter, both prominent citizens of Bern, Switzerland, enlist Lawson's help to convince our Baron to move here.

"What does Esquire mean Nana?"

"When the title 'Esquire' comes after a name, a man, or a woman, it means they're attorneys," she answered.

"Adam, before they met our Baron, Michel, and Ritter had petitioned the Lords Proprietors for a large piece of land, but without any ties to England or to the Lords Proprietors; basically they were trying to start their own independent country and of course the Lords Proprietors refused.

"Then they tried to obtain a land grant for their company on April 28, 1709. The minutes of that meeting say the Lords Proprietors instructed Michel that one of the company's investors had to purchase 5,000 acres and become a Carolina Landgrave in order for the Ritter Company to obtain a grant for land in Carolina.

"Adam, I know we banished most of the information about all of that to the boring details section but it might help if we understand a little about life back then.

"Life was a struggle for the poor, there was no government Welfare, Medicaid, Medicare, Social Security, or labor laws protecting children like we have now. Some who lived in cities worked and lived inside the factories and not in an apartment either, whole families would live crowded together along the walls beside the machinery, where even kids your age worked twice as long as workers do today and under horrible, dangerous conditions.

"Adam you could go to debtors' prison for not paying your bills, even the smallest amount would keep you in prison until it was paid so it's easy to understand why people were under a lot of pressure to make enough money just to keep body and soul together.

"Of course, it's not right but it's easy to understand how some might be less than honest and might try to manipulate people and situations to further their own careers.

"Like the rascals who played our poor Baron, beginning with the Lords Proprietors. The Crown had chided them for not doing more to attract settlers and although they knew Carolina was in rebellion and their government had collapsed they sill made the requirement that one of the Ritter Company become a Landgrave and buy 5,000 acres. Which at that time Adam was nearly as good as a death sentence.

"Lawson wanted to publish his book in London and he left Bath on February 9, 1709 and traveled to Hampton, Virginia to catch a ship going to England.

"Lawson probably arrived in England around the time Michel received the Lords Proprietors instruction that a member of the Ritter Company had to become a Carolina Landgrave.

"Nana paused for a moment gathering her thoughts to explain, "Adam not only that but other important events were also happening and opening a path which made it possible for our Baron to come here on his American adventure, after he finished his term as lieutenant governor of Yverdon, Switzerland

"England's Queen Anne only wanted volunteers to settle in her America colonies and in 1709 Queen Anne's *Golden Book* was published, urging the 'poor Palatines' who were seeking religious freedom, to let her help them. That she would pay for their passage to her colonies in America.

"Soon ten thousand refugees came to England and the queen needed help, and was willing to pay for taking her 'poor Palatines' off her hands and it is this career opportunity that would have unexpected consequences that changed our Baron's life.

"It was around this time that Lawson's book is also being published. Three hundred years later, when I checked out *A New Voyage to Carolina* from our library, I was able to read it enlightened by facts I learned during our research. To me it seemed as if his book was a big brochure for the rascal's 'Summer-Land Real Estate Development Swindle', which is the name I gave to it," confessed Nana with a little smile for Adam, so he would know she was being facetious.

"When Michel meets up with Lawson, they decide to convince our Baron to settle in Carolina instead of Virginia, to become a Carolina Landgrave and found a colony with hundreds of the 'poor Palatines' the Queen promised to help.

"The Queen doesn't care if her 'poor Palatines' go to Virginia or Carolina, both are her colonies and either way she'll pay for their passage.

"The Lords Proprietors care because they want a lot more settlers in Carolina who will be under the control of a Landgrave who will be loyal to them and of course because of the money they hope to make.

"Adam I think our Baron cares because he likes the idea of being a member of Carolina's royalty. You know that his father is a Baron in Switzerland and our Baron always struggled for his father's respect, so on August 4, 1709, he pays the Lords Proprietors 50 pounds sterling for 5,000 acres and becomes a Carolina Landgrave and Baron of Bernburg instead of a plantation owner in Virginia.

"I think it's interesting that the next entry in the same minutes records a 20 pounds sterling payment to Lawson for a copy of his Carolina map, which is apparently a lot of money, and shows that Lawson was also at that meeting with our Baron and Michel.

"Adam I think both Michel and Lawson care if the colony is in Carolina. One important reason, as far as Lawson is concerned, is that Lawson isn't the Surveyor General for Virginia, but he stands to gain a whole lot of money if they move to Carolina where he is the Surveyor General, and it is this business opportunity for Lawson that our Baron says he thought Lawson wanted him to choose Carolina.

"The contract with the Lords Proprietors and the Queen, to care for the Palatines, has Esquire after both our Baron's and Michel's names, and because Michel is an attorney there's no doubt that Michel knew what was what.

"There're several records of our Baron's meeting with the Lords Proprietors and its eerie reading when you know what's going to happen Adam.

"On the University of NC at Chapel Hill's website, *Documenting the American South*, I read about how our Baron met with Michel, who, by the way, had already wormed himself into a partner share of the Ritter Company in exchange for his 'pretend' silver mines in Virginia.

"It's about this same time that they realize our Baron has a lot more influence at court than Ritter and Michel combined and they talk our Baron into buying the land.

"Our Baron said he was leery at first, especially about the silver mines. That is until Michel introduced Lawson to our Baron as his longtime friend and as Carolina's Surveyor

General, so of course Lawson's opinion held a lot of weight when he vouched for Michel.

"Adam, on August 4, 1709, the Lords Proprietors conferred upon Christopher Graffenried the titles Landgrave of Carolina and Baron of Bernburg, in accordance with Carolina's Fundamental Constitutions. From then on all official documents refer him as 'Baron Christoph von Graffenried.'"

"That is also the reason that the ones who have been swindling the Lords Proprietors and the Queen want our Baron dead. They know he has sworn loyalty to the Queen and to Carolina's Lords Proprietors and that he is a man of his word; they all risk losing their heads if our Baron and the new governor Hyde succeed in restoring order and control back under the Lords Proprietors. What the rascals want are the settlers and their votes.

"Before our Baron even arrives in Carolina, political rabble-rousers are already at work enflaming the settlers, chanting 'Down with the Landgraves...!'"

"Down With the Landgraves...!"

"The Lords Proprietors were almost as bad as the other rascals Adam, insisting on having a Landgrave, taking our Baron's money, but not giving him a heads-up about the situation he was going into.

"I read all about it online and in that old 1925 school book *Young People's History of North Carolina*," declared Nana. There was a pamphlet in Documenting the South's Colonial and State Records, Volume 2 pages 891-923; *Party-Tyranny; or, An Occasional Bill In Miniature; As now Practiced in Carolina,* by Daniel Defoe that he presented to the Houses of Parliament, in London in1705.

"That means the Lords Proprietors, Lawson, Michel, Moseley, Cary and the other rascals all knew about the anarchy, and the commotions, and the mobs chanting 'Down with the Landgraves…' and why it seems to me that the Lords Proprietors threw our Baron and his hundreds of Palatines 'to the 'wolves' to test the mobs ugly mood.

"Adam, there really was a 'rascally gang', as our Baron called them, and it was made up of ruthless men. They were the ones involved in spreading lies about our Baron, for months before he even got here. They were even busy riling up the Palatines who had arrived with Lawson, trying to get them to join in the rebellion and to refuse to live according to Carolina's Fundamental Constitution.

"I won't go into all of that because, as you know it's all in the boring details section, but you do need to know a little or else you miss a lot of the pieces that make up the important back-story that reveals the big picture.

"It's no wonder the rascals threatened our Baron's whole colony and tried to starve them to death and wanted our Baron dead and even tried to kill him. A Landgrave with about 450 tenants that had survived the trip to live in New Bern was a real threat to the rascals, which is why Cary threatened them all if they sided with the Lords Proprietors and Governor Hyde.

"It made me sad when I read our Baron's contracts. The first one with the Queen was for a grant of land to settle on the south side of the Potomac River in Virginia and as a tenant of the Queen, instead of the Lords Proprietors.

"Where he would have been close to Williamsburg and the more civilized life there; he might not have been a Landgrave or a Baron Adam, but there is no doubt he would have become a successful plantation owner in America and most likely would have been very happy.

"Not long after returning to Bern, Switzerland our Baron wrote, in his defense, about his 'sad American adventures' and how his best laid plans failed because of 12 misfortunes. You can read his manuscript and see his map for the layout of New Bern in North Carolina's colonial archives.

"The town of Yverdon, Switzerland, where he had been lieutenant governor before moving here, sent a delegation to Raleigh, North Carolina to make an official copy of our Baron's manuscript for the lieutenant governor of Yverdon; you can go to Yverdon's official website and read their translation online.

"Adam, I thought it was interesting that our Baron is an important historical person in another city's history and it's their translation of our Baron's manuscript I read.

"It begins: 'The Commission of the Public Library of Yverdon certified that narration is the authentic copy made, of the manuscript titled: Number 3110. Account of a voyage to America in the year 1710, by a former lieutenant governor of Yverdon, a manuscript of 105 pages verified by them July 25 1885'.

"The last line our Baron wrote in his manuscript says: 'What I have experienced myself as may be seen above in the narration of the plot that was laid against me by a rascally gang'.

"Adam our Baron wrote that just as he was beginning to realize the different motivations of all those involved and how he had been duped. However, he did not know the half of it and he never learned how the rascals had really played him and the Lords Proprietors.

"Hardly anyone else knew either, because the rascals controlled then stole almost all of Carolina's records. Many of the ones who knew something about what had happened had died from smallpox or during the Indian Wars and many of the survivors had moved away.

"Thanks to our state's historians most of the records have been restored and published in twenty-six volumes as The Colonial and State Records of North Carolina. It took twenty-two years, between 1886 and 1907, to collect the copies of Carolina's colonial records from the governments of foreign countries and other states, libraries, museums, and individuals.

"Now we can read what the rascals did, so when some say Lawson should be credited with co-founding New Bern I wonder on what facts do they base that presumption.

"Especially if you start at the beginnings and learn about Lawson, his friends, and their swindles. You can understand why our Baron called them a 'rascally gang' and why the Indians wanted to torture Lawson to death.

"Adam, a rascal is a dishonest unscrupulous person, a real villain.

"The written agreement made with the Lords Proprietors and the Queen for the transportation and care of the 'poor Palatines' was with both our Baron and Michel. Both had equal responsibility providing for the colony. Even though our Baron paid Lawson for some of his land and Lawson was suppose to be a friend of Michel's, Lawson never invested in the colony.

"I think that's probably another clue Adam, because Lawson knew what a Carolina Landgrave was going to be up against, and he knew that our Baron's Swiss colony would not be a good investment.

"In the library book that Mr. Green suggested for you there was a copy of that very first map of New Bern.

"Our Baron wrote that it was the plan for the Swiss colony in Carolina and he dated it October 1710. He also includes Michel's full name with his name, but not Lawson's.

"They should research the colonial records housed at the University of North Carolina at Chapel Hill's libraries, and the Joyner Library in Greenville.

"There they can read all about what happened, and learn for themselves the real reason one year and eleven days after the founding of New Bern, the Indians kidnapped our Baron and Lawson and stuck Lawson full of splinters before setting him on fire and going on the warpath. Though they held our Baron a prisoner while they waged war they treated him well and freed him, which they would have done even without the letter from Governor Spotswood demanding his release.

"They can also learn the truth about how our Baron came face to face with that rascally gang. How he dealt with the treachery and tragedies while in the middle of mayhem created by sickness, revenge, greed and that Indian war that burned most of New Bern to the ground. Causing more than one observer to say that, 'northern Carolina was almost a wilderness, again'.

"Or they can just read about it in the boring details section, Nana," said Adam, smiling.

"That's true, Adam, but can you imagine how fierce the Native Indian warriors looked with war-paint on their faces and bodies when they went on the warpath for 3 days, riding up an down Middle Street and Union Point and all around the plantations. Can you imagine their blood-curling war cries and the screams of terror as the Indians tortured and killed one hundred and forty settlers; I will not go into any details about the way they tortured and killed them because it might give you nightmares.

"Our Baron even wrote about talking to one of the boys from New Bern who was your age. After the Indians had murdered his parents, they brought him back with them to the same camp where they were holding our Baron prisoner.

He said he admired a lot about the Indians Adam, but he also said that 'the worst thing about the Indians was their anger, it was 'fierce'.

"In fact, our Baron was lucky he got out of here alive!"

"Choose Your Friends Wisely; They Can Get You Killed!"

"The assassin's leader put tongs into the fire until it was glowing red," spoke Adam in a quite voice tone; casting a glance at Nana, his voice trailed off into silence, unsure if he should continue telling the story.

Curious, Nana said, "When metal changes color like that it's called 'red-hot', then what happened?"

"When it was red-hot," continued Adam, "the leader took the tongs out of the fire and burned another assassin with it while other members held him down."

Seeming bewildered that people would participate in such cruelty Adam added, "The game also has an assassin's code Nana and that's probably why they did it, since they were all assassins. Maybe he was being punished for not following orders to assassinate someone."

"What kind of game is that," Nana questioned?

"It's a video game where the assassin tries to kill and he has different tricks. One trick is to throw money into the air over a group of people so the assassin can escape," replied Adam, pronouncing the words with an Italian accent, adding, "I said it like that Nana because that's how they pronounced the words in the game. They are in cities named Venice, Rome, and Florence where they speak Italian.

"Well at least you're learning a little geography and you do have a great Italian accent but you should understand something about violent games like that.

"In real life, even if they escape and seem to get away with it, eventually they'll suffer the consequences and will pay for it in the afterlife, because there's a lot more to life than this visible world."

"I know, Nana, it is Karma."

"You are correct," said Nana. "One definition of Karma could be 'what goes around comes back around' and that's why the wise conclude that 'the eye that does not see the spirit world is to be considered no better than the eye of a peacock's feather, beautiful but blind'.

"Adam, that game is inspired by criminal activity and there could be dangerous consequences for some players, in this world and the next, who might be lured into thinking that since they arc good at the game they would be good at it in real life.

"Can you see how throwing silver mines and titles into the deal with our Baron are good examples of that assassin's trick of distraction when they throw money into the air?"

"Yes," Adam replied. "But I wish the silver mines had been real Nana. If the silver mines had been real I do not think our Baron would have gone back to Bern because he would have had all of the money he needed."

"You might be right, Adam and that makes me wonder:

"What if everything happened according to plan and there had been no misfortunes.

"What if our Baron's real estate partners had been reliable and performed what they agreed to do in their written contracts with him.

"What if everyone arrived here safe and over three hundred Palatines had not died on the way to New Bern.

"What if pirates had not robbed the Palatines just before their ship landed.

"What if Lawson had not lied and there was not a Neusiok Indian village in the way and Lawson had settled them where he should have, so they could have cleared their own land, instead of Lawson's.

"What if there had been no Fundamental Constitution and instead of being a Landgrave our Baron just another plantation owner and a real estate developer who brought hundreds of tenants with him

"What if there had been no land swindles and the settlers had been good neighbors to the Indians.

"What if, from the very beginning, everyone had followed that Golden Rule and treated one another like they wanted to be treated.

"Adam would your hometown be any different, or better, if everything had happened according to plan, because there really is a big difference between a wild time and a good time; greed and revenge can drive people wild and good-will can lead to good-things.

"You should learn two lessons from games like that, Adam.

"The first lesson teaches you about friends because there really are people in this world with evil intentions. They are willing to do anything in order to achieve their ends and use fear of violence to force respect and obedience.

"Blackbeard is a good example. Once, he was sitting around with his mates, when all of a sudden he deliberately shot his own first mate in the knee, crippling him for life. When his mate asked why he shot him, Blackbeard told him he wanted to shoot one of them ever so often so they would not forget who he was.

"That is the first lesson: You must choose your friends wisely; they can get you killed!

"Adam, George Washington is quoted as giving this good advice to a nephew and I wish to pass his advice on to you; 'Be courteous to all; intimate with few'."

"You said there were two lessons Nana, what is the second?" asked Adam.

"The second lesson is important because it is a warning," explained Nana.

"The second lesson: If something seems too good to be true, beware."

Then, throwing a hand full of papers into the air over Adam's head Nana ran out of the room shouting, "Free money run for your life!"

Our Baron's Bust Is Not a Bust of Our Baron

"Google Christoph V von Graffenried, Adam. When you use the German style of writing his name you will get many different results than when you Google Christopher de Graffenried V.

"On the 'Plan of New Bern' map that our Baron made you can see that he wrote his name using the German style, von Graffenried, but when he went back to Switzerland he wrote his name de Graffenried, using the French style which is the way Swiss nobility did it back then."

"Nana, maybe that's because almost everyone was German so he wrote it in German so they could read it, because I can't read I," Adam said.

"I can't read it either," admitted Nana. "But I did look up 'de' and 'von' in the dictionary which explains that both the French 'de' and the German 'von' stand for place of origin and also implies royalty.

"What have we here?" Nana asked, pointing to a web

address with the cursor. "Look, some of these websites are in England and Switzerland. Let's go to Switzerland Adam and visit the de Graffenried family's website," suggested Nana, while giving it a quick double click with the mouse.

Nana could hardly believe what appeared on the computer screen "Adam, sit here and read this, but read it out loud, please."

"OK," agreed Adam, "MsDeG: FROM WORB NEAR BERN, SWITZERLAND TO NEW BERN, NORTH CAROLINA, USA—The American Adventures of Christoph V von Graffenried."

Looking up from the computer Adam asked, "Nana what does that mean?"

"It seems 'MsDeG' stands for a female de Graffenried who lives in Worb, Switzerland, that's where the Graffenried castle is located and where our Baron lived.

"MsDeG is saying that she has set up this website to share with New Bern our Baron's American adventure story and information about the de Graffenried families who live in the United States now. What else does she say?"

Apparently, Adam had been reading ahead because all of a sudden, raising his voice, he exclaimed, "It's not even him! Nana, she said that the bust of our Baron is not our Baron!"

"What are you talking about, Adam, how can the bust of our Baron not be our Baron? That doesn't make any sense," concluded Nana.

"She said that when New Bern wanted to make that bust of our Baron they couldn't find any pictures of him so they gave them a picture of one of his relatives they thought might look like him.

"But what I want to know," Adam wondered out loud, "is how they can know that. The ones that sent the picture couldn't know if he looked like our Baron, that picture has to be as old as New Bern because she says that the man in the picture died in 1719," complained Adam, outraged at the trick played on him.

"I really believed it was our Baron when you took my picture with it, Nana," declared Adam with a crestfallen look.

"Who knows Adam, maybe he does look like our Baron, maybe not. I know that a lot of people have family resemblances," Nana said, trying to sooth his feelings of betrayal.

"But only twins would look like each other and they definitely are not twins," retorted Adam still upset.

"Maybe they were thinking that the resemblance comes from the way they dressed, maybe our Baron did dress like that, we know he wore a wig because our Baron told about when they were prisoners the Indians took his and Lawson's wigs and threw them into the fire. That's probably how his wig looked but maybe his face was different. People did say our Baron was tall and handsome."

"Yes, but it's still not true!" insisted Adam. "Now every time I see that picture of his relative, or our Baron's bust , or that picture of the bust at McDonald's®, or go downtown and actually see the bust, I will not ever be able to look at them again without thinking that I am really looking at a stranger that never came here."

"I have an idea, we can take a picture of you with Bearon de Graffenried," suggested Nana, trying to change the subject. "Some of our Baron's relatives, including Betty Woods Thomas who is our Baron's 6th generation granddaughter, attended the ceremony when they unveiled the Bearon de Graffenried statue at Union Point Park. I've read many stories she wrote for the Sun Journal about our Baron and New Bern's history.

"While we're at Union Point Park we can read what our Baron had to say. We know he roamed all around where the Bearon de Graffenried statue stands because that is where he lived in his cabin.

"Adam, we should consider this as an important reminder about why we should do our own research because sometimes what we take for history is really a bunch of lies."

Sometimes History Gives Good Advice, Sometimes It Lies

"Nana, if our Baron did the right thing why was he sad?" quizzed Adam, his wrinkled brow showing a little puzzled concerned.

"We can tell from our Baron's letters to his son and the story he wrote about his American adventure that he believed in God and it was his belief in God that led him to follow the Golden Rule.

"Listen and I'll try to explain to you what our Baron said about his belief in God and the effect it had on him and why he did what he did when he lived in New Bern.

"Many times in our Baron's life, even before he came to America, he said he felt responsible for the people in his care and had tried to do the right thing even when it was at great personal cost, and that he prayed for God to put into his mind what he should do.

"Our Baron was in a real-life and a very dangerous game of politics and intrigue."

"Nana, what does intrigue mean?" asked Adam.

"Intrigue can mean appealing to people's interest in an unusual or compelling way but also can be defined as trying to accomplishing that goal by being deceitful and using underhanded methods, which is the meaning here.

"In their letters and in the minutes of their meetings, Virginia's Governor and the Lords Proprietors referred to the events our Baron found himself in as 'disorders', 'confusions', and 'commotions', all stirred into motion by intrigue.

"First let me tell you what those words mean Adam, because in official government documents words are carefully chosen and should be considered meaningful.

"'Disorders' refer to a civil unrest of disorderly conduct and fighting that interrupts the public peace.

"'Confusions' refer to a brawl, creating upheaval, to defeat, overthrow, or ruin.

"'Commotions' refer to the violent noisy disturbance of a riot as a political or social rebellion against an established government.

"The point is that not only are the rascals real so are the records that prove our Baron wasn't wrong when he called them a 'rascally gang'. We are talking real intrigue Adam, because their necks were on the line they would stop at nothing and being deceitful and underhanded was the least of it. In one way or another they are ruthless political rabble-rousers; they are the ones who are responsible for most of the disorders, confusions, and commotions all around here.

"Adam what happened during the first two years after the founding of your hometown seems like the plot of an adventure action movie with a rascally gang out to kill our Baron, a rioting mob out to kill Landgraves, Indians on the warpath out to kill the settlers, and starvation driving our Baron to desperate measures.

"The Tuscarora Indian War left Carolina unable to help New Bern and Virginia and South Carolina couldn't help anymore than they already had and during the war, that's when our Baron decided that going to England to personally report and to appeal to the Queen and the Lords Proprietors for help was his last and only resort.

"On the way to England, our Baron first stopped in Virginia to meet Governor Spotswood and he was shocked when the governor realized that our Baron was not aware of what was really going on, he filled our Baron in, telling him as much as he dared. That is when our Baron began to realize how Michel and Lawson had played him.

"Adam, I'm sad to say that instead of finding help in England our Baron only finds more misfortunes. He finds that his most important supporter, Queen Anne, is suffering from dropsy and her heir and their ministers know she is deathly ill and she dies on August 1, 1714. He finds that other friends at court were dead or out of favor and he is unable to obtain an audience with the new king-in-waiting who already had so many serious concerns that a far away little Swiss colony could not be a priority.

"Once our Baron discoverers that New Bern was not a priority for England or for his unfaithful partners in Switzerland, and realizing that he had to accept defeat he went back home, ashamed.

"Our Baron said he regretted not buckling down and studying harder when he was a student in school and thought that if he had he would have been more successful in his career.

"Since he knew he wouldn't have the blessings of his domineering father he had left on his American adventure in secret causing some to complain that he failed his family, but in reality Adam he left them safe and well taken care of and he had left with high hopes of making them proud of him. He is depressed because he could not satisfy the expectations of his tenants, friends, family, business partners, nor himself.

"But no serious historian can deny that our Baron tried his

best, followed the Golden Rule, and fought the Good Fight, and in doing so he sacrificed his wealth, his future, his reputation, everything, in order to do the right thing for New Bern.

"He should not have felt guilty, nor thought he was a failure, nor been ashamed and sad because, in spite of it all, the true story shows how our Baron prayed for guidance from God and asked for God to put into his mind what he should do.

"When I look at our Baron's American adventure I see that even though he wanted to make everything perfect and he tried his best, he was at the wrong place at the wrong time.

"In reality Adam, I believe that God rewarded our Baron's heroic efforts, sending him back home, to Switzerland, to a retired life of quite contemplation, which is a blessing in old age.

"God also exposed to our Baron his false friends and partners who libeled him to cover up their own misdeeds and failures.

"He should have been glad not be bothered by them anymore and not been sad because he knew he tried his best to do the right thing and that should be good enough for anyone.

The Seventh Journey is to the North Carolina Regional History Center

The History of the History Center

"I have a surprise for you Adam. Since you are out of school today, I have made plans for us to go on the last journey of your adventure into history.

"I hope you're going to agree with me that there's no better place to end your adventure than going downtown to visit the new North Carolina Regional History Center (HC).

"Adam, since the HC is only seven months old, this was a good time to research how the HC came to be in New Bern.

"Before we visit any of the exhibits, I want to tell you what I learned about the history of the HC.

"I see that smile, but I'm serious, I'm not trying to play an April Fool's Day joke on you. I really did research the history of the HC."

Laughing, Adam said, "It's not that Nana. I'm laughing because I think the 'history of the HC' sounds funny."

"I knew you'd like that play on words, but I think you'll like the story even more and I think it will help you appreciate the HC, because there's more to it's exhibits than meets the eye.

"And New Bern is lucky it was built here so, please, don't banish it to the boring details section. Okay?"

"Okay," promised Adam, trying hard to look serious.

Standing in front of the entrance of the HC, while Nana got her camera ready to take his picture, Adam commented, "Nana, I was just thinking that we started on my adventure into history when I was five years old and now I'm 9 years old, it sure took us a long time."

"Research takes time Adam, but I'm sure we'll still go on a lot of other adventures. After all, there's a whole lot more to do around here than time traveling into the past.

"Oh, snap!" exclaimed Nana. "Stay there Adam. I moved the camera before it took your picture and accidently took a picture of the parking lot.

"On second thought, maybe it's a lucky accident. I know they made the parking lot out of special materials that allows rainwater to flow through it. Don't you think that was a clever idea?"

"Yes, and now I really do want to hear the story."

"Back up a little bit Adam, I want to get a picture of you with the clock over the doors to the building. It shows that you were here at 11:40 a.m. on April 1, 2011 and. I can see the words 'NORTH CAROLINA HISTORY CENTER' reflected in the windows over the doors.

"Adam the HC is already interesting and we haven't even made it inside, yet."

Inside, a woman standing behind the ticket counter greeted them with a friendly smile saying "Welcome to the North Carolina History Center. How may I help you, today?"

Nana replied, "Mrs. Gulley, I don't know if you remember me, but I want to thank you for suggesting that I talk to Mr. Dean Knight. You were right. He was able to tell me the interesting story about the founding of the HC.

"This is my grandson, Adam. Before we visit the exhibits I want to pass on that story to him over lunch at Lawson's Landing Riverwalk Café."

Nana started walking towards the café, but Adam stopped her saying, "Wait Nana, you have to look at the giant clock that's on the wall over the doors."

"Wow! That certainly is an impressive clock, Adam and I have never seen a pendulum like that before; it looks like it could reverse time. Don't you think it was a great idea to exhibit such an unusual clock in a museum where you can go time-traveling?"

"Not if the pendulum falls off and hits someone on the head Nana. Look at it! It looks dangerous. There's nothing under it to keep it from falling if whatever is holding it up there breaks. Maybe they should put a shelf under it and a sign with the date up there, too," suggested Adam. "Then when visitors leave the HC they'll know the pendulum can't fall on them and that this portal takes them to the present world."

"I don't believe that you have to worry about the pendulum falling on people. A Sun Journal reporter, Charlie Hall, wrote a story in the Sun Journal about how a famous clockmaker, Seth Thomas, made that clock 100 years ago, that it weighs 2,800 pounds, that pendulum you see is 8-1/2 feet long, and the bob on the end weighs 325 pounds.

"Adam that's the original clock that hung in the tower on top of New Bern's Town Hall, but after a hundred years it started breaking down and needed to be rebuilt. New Bern got a new modern clock and donated that valuable Seth Thomas clock so that it could be on display here.

"Over the years I must have looked at that clock a thousand times when it was in the tower. Then you could only see the clock's face and it was a beautiful sight at night with the red dots of light all around the face, appearing to be illuminated rubies.

"Mr. Hall wrote that it took 12 volunteers working almost every Saturday for 4 years to restore it. Now, it works great and still strikes the time, and don't worry, they know how to hang things properly here, this is a museum after all and that's an important part of what they do.

"I can see what you are talking about though," Nana said. "It does look heavy, but it's supposed to hang like that. I don't think that there's ever been any report of the pendulum falling off, and we can always leave through the patio exit so that it can't fall on us. That is, if you're still worried," teased Nana.

Nana glanced at her cell phone and said, "Look at the time Adam, it's almost 12:00. Did you see that! Just as the time on my phone changed to 12:00, we heard the first strike."

The clock was still chiming out the hour when Adam opened the door to the café for Nana saying "Yes, and I'm definitely glad we're still in the present, because I'm hungry, Nana. I think I'd like to order a salad and a root beer-float."

After ordering lunch, they looked around and Nana remarked, "I don't think it really matters where you sit Adam, in every direction the living wetlands scenery makes me want to come here often.

"Adam, I imagine they recreated the wetlands along the bank of the Trent River here to show how this place must have looked when the Indians lived here.

"See that tall bridge, way across the water in front of us, it crosses over the Trent River. On this side, the Trent River joins with the Neuse River and that is why they named that spit of land Union Point.

That's where our Baron's cabin would have been, to our right, and behind those trees way down this side of the bank, do your see that tall white building?"

"Yes, ma'am," answered Adam.

"That's the same building we saw across the creek when we were at Lawson Creek Park and I told you that's where Lawson Street ends and where Lawson had his cabin. Now you can see how close together they all were.

"Adam, we definitely have to come back soon and explore the outside of the HC, but today let's concentrate on the inside. I think the window walls are brilliant; they turned out to be more than windows.

"Don't you love the way the windows wrap around the HC, almost from the ceiling to the floor? Across the patio you can see the outside of more windows and they appear to be covered with a transparent animated poster of a beautiful river scene?"

"Yes," Adam agreed, "And I also like the inside windows. It's almost like being outside."

"Adam, I really like the decorative green squares running around the upper borders. I think it's sea-green, what color would you call it?"

"I think sea-green has more turquoise in it, Nana, like teal does. I think the color is a minty-green, and it's transparent so I would call it a ghostly-minty-green."

"That's a very interesting name for a color, Adam, especially when you remember that this café was named after Lawson, the green squares could represent his ghost, floating along the ceiling."

Laughing, Adam suggested, "Let's name the color of the windows Lawson's ghostly green."

"I like that idea Adam, and it reminds me why we are here. I really do want to tell you about the history of the HC story. Once upon a time, two weeks ago," Nana began, earning a chuckle from Adam she added, "I was just making sure you're listening."

"I'm listening Nana, I really do want to hear this history story."

"Good and it really was just a couple of weeks ago that I met with Mr. Dean Knight, who is one of seven curators who work for the Tryon Palace organization (TP). His title is Curator for Collections Research and Interpretation. I explained I thought the story about the history of the HC would make the perfect ending for your adventure into the history of your hometown and he agreed to tell me the story about the founding of the HC.

"Just to make certain that you know, a curator is someone who is in charge of a museum or museum collections; they manage and supervise everything, including restoring and preserving items in a museum's collections, and what, and why, and how, to exhibit them."

Wanting to point out a challenge they would need to be good at Adam said, "I hope that includes knowing how to hang them up so they can't fall onto people."

Getting a smile from Nana, she replied, "I'm certain they were taught how to hang an artifact so that it would not fall Adam, but if I had known of your concerns I would have asked Mr. Knight how they hang heavy objects. He told me many other things, though, and I want to pass them on so that when we go through the HC galleries we can remember what he said. Then, we will not only enjoy seeing the exhibits but we'll also be able to better appreciate how they're being displayed and the stories they tell."

"Nana, do you think they'll have that fake picture of our Baron that the lady on the de Graffenried website said wasn't really our Baron, but a picture of one of his relatives?"

"Well, it's not a question of 'if' they display the picture that was used to make the bust of our Baron, what counts is what they say about it. Remember, curators are responsible for researching an artifact before they make an interpretation about it," said Nana, adding, "I know you'll be looking for that picture!"

"And you would be correct!" he replied, while nodding 'yes', leaving no doubt about it.

"I began my interview by asking Mr. Knight why they changed the name of Tryon Palace to the Governor's Palace, but still use the words 'Tryon Palace' on banners flying around the HC building.

"Mr. Knight explained that when the HC was added they thought they should 'rebrand' the Tryon Palace organization because the historical experience had expanded beyond having the palace as the centerpiece.

"Now there's the HC, the Governor's Palace, the Gardens, the historical homes around the palace, and the Academy Museum.

"The use of the Tryon Palace name still seemed a little

confusing to me so when I got home I did more research, online.

"The General Statutes of North Carolina (1973, c. 476, s. 54.), explains how the Tryon Palace Historic Sites and Gardens was formed.

"That it would operate, under a Director, who would oversee the overall business operations of the Tryon Palace Historic Sites and Gardens, but would do so under the guidance of the Tryon Palace Commission of the Department of Cultural Resources (TPC) and under the overall supervision of the Director of the Division of Archives and History.

"Everything remains under the supervision of the TPC, which explains why 'Tryon Palace' (TP).remains included in its name, and on its website, its referred to as Tryon Palace. org.

"Of course, Mr. Knight pointed-out that Governor Tryon was the one who had the palace built, but he wasn't the only governor to live there and it would be more historically correct to rename Tryon Palace the Governor's Palace (GP)."

Adam said "The GP is a better name for the palace, Nana; some people probably though the Tryon family still lived there."

"You could be right and I can see how the old name could confuse tourists," admitted Nana. "He also said that visitors often asked the palace staff why the building was named Tryon Palace and that now they don't have to explain all of that anymore and can concentrate on telling about the palace's history as the first permanent capitol of North Carolina (NC).

"Just think, the HC has only been open for 7 months, but Mr. Knight told how it took a lot of nameless people working together for 12 years to create, this is a quote Adam, 'a 21st century, hands-on, state-of-the-art HC that would exhibit

10,000 years of history.' I know, that is a mouthful to say, Adam, but I wanted you to know what a big job TPC gave the TP staff.

"It's not hard to see why they needed a lot of talented experts to help them if they wanted to achieve something superexcellent and beneficial for New Bern and NC.

"The reason I said 'nameless people' was because Mr. Knight repeatedly pointed out that it wasn't because of the efforts of one person that the HC became a reality. I think Mr. Knight wanted us to know that what was important was their expertise, not their names, because an expert is someone who knows a great deal about something and uses their knowledge to solve problems and to take advantage of opportunities.

"He explained that it wasn't just TP experts that achieved the goal, either, because they had big plans, it took the cooperation of many experts from other museums, universities, government agencies, and companies all working together.

"When you think about everything that was involved you quickly realize that creating the HC was a very complicated and a huge undertaking. It included everything from underground to the tops if the buildings, and everything inside and outside, including the air, and the rivers and creeks.

Placing some papers on the table, she said, "I don't want to leave out anything so I brought the notes I took during my interview with Mr. Knight.

"First he explained how internally there was always the TP staff, and he rattled of a long list of experts that they invited to help them.

Then Nana began reading aloud from her notes:

"Outside scholars, who are expert in our local history and regional culture, from the University of NC and other universities; foresters, from the US Department of Forestry;

scientists from the US Environmental Protection Agency and other scientists; staff from the NC Office of Archives and History, the Department of Cultural Resources (NCOAHDCR); building and landscape architects and all the people needed to construct the building and landscape; electricians, expert in special affects lighting; expert and innovative plumbers; computer and interactive media experts; creative and talented artisans, like silversmiths and blacksmiths; restoration experts; and expert designers and fabricators, to design and build the exhibits."

"That's a lot of people," declared Adam. "It could've been hundreds or even thousands of people Nana, and I think that's probably one of the reasons he didn't want to use names."

"I'm certainly glad he concentrated on teamwork, instead," confessed Nana, "that would have been a lot of names to type.

"Mr. Knight said that it all began in 1998 when an opportunity came to buy the Barbour Boat Works (BBW), which had closed a few years earlier.

"The moment the TPC learned the BBW property was for sale they knew they needed to buy it, because it was so close to the palace and it would give them a way to expand.

"One of the reasons they needed to expand was to have space to finally display the large amount of stored artifacts they owned, but didn't quite fit in with the historical theme of the palace, so they were never able to display them.

"But they had no idea how that would happen, Adam."

"I don't think they knew it would take 12 years, either, Nana."

"I think you're right, and I don't think anyone could even guess what they would be up against, or what they would be able to accomplish.

"I'll go ahead and say right up-front that New Bern was blessed when TPC decided to buy the BBW property.

"The HC is finished, so it's easy to say that now, because people can see for themselves how it turned out.

"I know you'll be proud to learn that the HC and GP are accredited museums of the NCOAHDCR, and that the HC received the Leadership in Environmental and Energy Design (LEED) Silver certification, as a green-designed project.

"But back to the beginning of the story. It was about 1998 when the TP Director, Kay Williams, set everything in motion by creating an ad hoc committee."

"What does ad hoc mean, Nana?"

"That the committee has a specific purpose to consider, this committee's special purpose was to work on a proposal to buy the BBW.

"It took a long time because they weren't just buying property; they were brainstorming and coming up with dozens of ideas for developing the property in their proposal.

"That's how the process began, and they decided that they wanted to build a regional history museum and a recreational area, and they grouped together with state offices including the NCOAHDCR.

"Once TP owned the property, Ms. Williams formed new committees, to ask for proposals and estimates to build the HC.

"Mr. Knight said it took many hours of meetings, by many different groups brainstorming up ideas about how to turn the property into the HC. They also had to develop the general outline of what stories to tell and what and how to display items from the stored collections, before they could narrow their focus and to prepare the groundwork on all of the different proposals they needed to ask for.

"They needed proposals to design and build the building, the landscaping, the lighting, the displays, the interactive multi-media displays that would have photographs and videos, right down to the color of the walls and the style of the doorknobs, I could go, but you get the idea.

"They also worked closely with several government agencies that I already told you about. For your sake, I won't go into how difficult that can be, since it involves laws, rules, regulations, and guidelines, and I know you'll wish you could banish it, so I'll just mention the Superfund.

"Adam the Superfund is the name of a government program created by the US Environmental Protection Agency (EPA). One of its goals is to help communities clean up hazardous waste sites like the BBW property, which had been polluting the Trent River and the Neuse River Basin for 55 years before it closed. Mr. Knight called it a 'Brownfield'.

"Google 'Superfund' and look up 'Brownfield' and you can get a glimpse of what the Superfund does. Even then, you can only get a tiny hint of how intimidating the job really was.

"It's easy to say 'cleanup a Brownfield', Adam, but the truth is it took a lot of effort and years to safely clean up the contaminated property and to restore it into the natural wetlands we are looking at right now.

"Of course the cleanup had to be done before they could even begin building or landscaping. Until then it was a dangerous, unhealthy mess, and an eyesore and an embarrassment for the community, especially when tourists visited the palace.

"It's important to understand what they were up against Adam, so I need to tell you a few of the things that I leaned from the Superfund website about Brownfields and green infrastructures.

"Adam, you're interested in becoming a scientist so you'll appreciate the science behind a Superfund site.

"Not only is the soil contaminated with chemicals but so is

the ground water and the underground air which can harm the health of people, animals, and plants there, or even if they just go near a Brownfield site. Just think about all of those years of contaminated run-off-water going into the Trent and Neuse Rivers, and nearby creeks and streams, polluting many miles of our waterways.

"There's a lot of science involved when cleaning up a Brownfield because they have to use a lot of different technologies in order to clean the contamination from the soil and the underground air and water, sometimes they even have to remove the contaminated soil, so there's no longer a threat to human health and the environment.

"Adam, we're talking about the fact that it's going to take heavy equipment like bulldozers, cranes, backhoes, soil filters, a gigantic cistern, and many other things in order to reclaim and reuse 16 acres of toxic land."

"Nana, maybe they had to dig out so much dirt that they decided to build a cistern in the big hole it left."

"Well, you have to admit that is certainly a clever way to fill up a big hole and a lot better than trying to fill the hole up with dirt from somewhere else. Can you just imagine those brainstorming meetings, when they came up with the cistern idea?"

"They had to be happy, Nana, because it's a great idea."

"It is a great idea Adam, and they probably needed several proposals since their goal was to transform an unhealthy mess into a healthy building site. I wouldn't be surprised if their committees had sub-committees."

"What if their sub-committees had to have sub-sub-committees, Nana?"

"I wouldn't be surprised at that either, Adam, because there was a lot to consider and do.

"For one thing, the EPA promotes the use of green infrastructure by cities and towns to reduce storm-water runoff, because it pollutes the local waterways, and a green infrastructure keeps polluted storm-water from entering the waterways or the community's sewer systems.

"The website claims that polluted storm-water is a nationwide challenge because it contaminates the habitats of many different species of animals and marine life that live in and around our waterways, and that it also increases the chance of flooding.

"Green infrastructure includes the use of permeable materials that allow water to flow through it so that rain-water can be captured, like the materials in our HC parking lot. After the water is capture, it passes through filters to clean pollutants from it, before they store in the cistern or reuse on site.

"Energy savings for the community is another benefit, because it keeps the storm-water from entering the storm-sewers so that it doesn't have to be processed at treatment plants.

"All of that helps us understand what they had to consider when they were brainstorming ideas on how to make the best of a bad situation. Especially, since they wanted to set a good example in our community by building an environmentally friendly 'green' project.

"Those brainstorming ideas resulted in the creation of the landscaping and the construction of wetlands to filter rainfall from 50-acres of the New Bern Historic District into the underground cistern

"Not only that, they also wanted the HC building to be 'green' and energy-efficient and when they were finished their efforts were recognized, earning the Silver Certification from the non-profit global organization, The Green Building Certification Institute, GBCI.

"Adam, even though it was a difficult undertaking they decided it was worth it, because there're many environmental and financial benefits when you go for LEED certification.

"It cost less to operate a 'green' building so it increases the value of the building, using recycled materials reduces landfill waste, and energy-efficiency reduces harmful greenhouse gas emissions into the environment, and saves energy and water.

"They earned the Silver Certification because the construction of the HC followed the LEED guidelines: for Water Efficiency, for Energy and Atmosphere control, for Indoor Environmental Quality (for instance the HC's window design saves electricity by using daylight lighting, instead of artificial lighting) and Innovation in Building Design.

"Implementing those guidelines pays off everyday for the HC because they increase the energy-efficiency of the heat and air conditioning and the mechanical and electrical equipment, helps the environment, creates a healthier place to work and to visit, and saves the HC money on utilities, including lights, water, and sewage.

"Those are just some of the many good reasons for wanting to be green, Adam, but the best reason is that it makes the HC a healthier place to visit and work, and why they were required to reserve a few parking spaces for 'green' cars. We should take a picture of the signs that say 'This Space is Reserved for Sustainable Sites-Low Emitting/ Fuel Efficient Vehicles' for your photo album.

"Adam, those spaces were selected because they're in front of the HC's entrance doors and will help reduce the amount of harmful pollution entering the building from car's carbon monoxide gas fumes.

"So you can see why I said they had big ideas and why they needed proposals from all of the different parts of the project, before they could even get to the point where they could decide on building a 60,000 square foot building and how to landscape the 16 acres of grounds.

"Then, after the deadline for receiving proposals, people from the TPC, the TP staff, and state officials from the NCOAHDCR grouped together to go over the proposals. After many committee meeting, and consultations with the experts and scholars, they selected the best proposals from the best companies.

"I asked Mr. Knight why they chose ESI Design (ESI). He said that ESI was already experienced in enriching the museum experience by backing it up using state-of-the-art interactive technology and they didn't want to make any costly mistakes by trying to figure it all out with an inexperienced company.

"I went home and Googled ESI and quickly realized what he meant and how lucky we are they chose ESI's proposal. It turns out, that ESI designed their first hands-on learning environment for the Brooklyn Children's Museum in 1977.

"ESI had designed other important projects, too, like the Ellis Island - American Family Immigration History Center. Adam, Ellis Island is where the Statue of Liberty is located and is one of America's most important landmarks.

"ESI also designed Sony Plaza and Sony Wonder Technology Lab, and many other projects and some have even won awards for their innovative, interactive designs that encourage visitors to participate.

"Mr. Knight said that it was about 2001-2002 before they got schematic drawings giving them their first concept of the building as it took shape on paper and they could see the square footage and the space they had to work with and they began raising money to build it.

"Mr. Knight said they received public and private donations

and even received donations from school kids who collected thousands of pennies for the project. When they had enough money, they started groundbreaking.

"That's when their efforts started to gel and they could decide on what stories to tell and what and how to exhibit the artifacts and what to eliminate and they decided they would not focus on any one individual. For example, they would focus not on just one or two women but on many women equally.

"That's also when the Cullman Performance Hall, the Duffy Exhibit Gallery, and the Pepsi Family Center developed as anchors for the HC.

"Of course, all that meant they needed more committees to carry the vision forward. In fact, Mr. Knight said every detail was important, even where the toilets would be located in the bathrooms."

Laughing Adam said, "Nana, I think that would be an interesting committee meeting."

"I think you're right," agreed Nana, "They probably had a few laughs, and they probably were careful where they hung the mirrors.

"It's about this same time that they developed a timeline for the museum, from about 10,000 years ago, to about 1950. Mr. Knight said they wanted to begin 'pre-contact', meaning before the Indians meet the Europeans, and they decided to narrow their focus to this region, of about sixteen counties, but stopping before Wake County and Raleigh, which is why they call it a regional HC.

"As they narrowed the focus, Mr. Knight said that's when the real work started for the TP staff, and when outside culture resources, scholars, foresters, and other experts vetted the collections.

Nana, answering Adam's question, explained, "Adam

vetted means that the experts appraises and verifies, or checks that the artifacts, manuscripts, and documents are not fakes and are accurately interpreted.

"Mr. Knight said he loves maps and that the HC has five of the best maps in the world."

"Does he know we made maps, Nana?"

"Yes, I took them with me, even thought they aren't quite camera ready. I wanted him to see the region you covered on your adventure. So I was glad he said he liked maps."

"I'm glad he likes maps too, Nana."

"Adam, it's at this point they decided on the designs and fabrications of the exhibits. They invited hundreds of artisans, professionals, and scholars, the best of the best, to help the TP staff make important decisions, about what artifacts to select and the stories they would tell and how to exhibit them.

"He said that it took weeks and weeks just to decide on the colors for the different exhibits and the backgrounds; how to mount artifacts, 'should they be on pedestals, or floating in air, or sit on the floor' and they started setting deadlines for photographs, life size cutouts, and other elements that would be used.

"They decided to use a blue trail on the floor, as a 'river of life' that you can follow into the past, every section leading you on a richer experience through time by using text panels, graphic panels, prints and interactive videos with actors.

"Then they brought in the design people to use attractive artistic representations to layer 3-D like displays- from murals on the walls, then adding cutouts of trees and scenes, including you-are-there scenes, created by using life-size cut-outs, to further enrich the visitor's experiences.

"There were also opportunities for pictorial representation through interactive visuals using videos and audios so you can go deeper and deeper into details, if you want to know more."

"Nana, do you mean that they have boring details sections, too?" quizzed Adam.

"I guess you could call them that. Mr. Knight said that you could have a rich experience just following the 'blue river of life', but you could choose to see and hear more if you wanted to have an even 'richer experience'.

"Adam, imagine we're flies on the wall during a committee meeting. We would see many people from all over the country, sitting around a large conference table-covered with architectural blueprints, drawings and maps and notebooks and pencils and pens and glasses and cups and there would be a lot more chairs arranged about the room, filled with participants and interested observers.

"During the development of a hand-held GPS history navigator, that you can rent, the members of the committee named it Argus.

"Mr. Knight said that you can use Argus to walk in the footsteps of history around the GP from the viewpoint of a child, a slave, an aristocrat, an artisan, or some other person you select, who tells you about what happened to them there.

"Ms. Gulley, the woman at the ticket booth, said you can rent it for $5.00 and that when you return it they refund your $50.00 deposit, but if you have a smart phone you can download the application for free from the TP website."

"What does 'Argus' mean, Nana? If all of those people are smart enough to invent a history navigator then they probably named it 'Argus' for a good reason."

"I think you might be onto something, Adam, but I don't know what Argus means, let's Google it.

"Adam, it seems there's a Greek myth about an all-seeing giant named Argus who has 100 eyes and his job was to guard a calf named Io. That he was a very effective guard, because 'sleep never fell upon his eyes and he was always a wakeful watcher.' The story ends when he dies, saying his eyes transferred onto the tails of peacocks.

"Adam, Argus is a GPS, which could be called a wakeful watcher, and you could even say that it's the guardian of an archived history library. Do you think that Mr. Knight might have told us that the navigator's creators named it Argus on purpose, you know, to see if we would research it, because the people in the HC call it 'The History Navigator'."

"Nana, I think he wanted to give us a clue, and if he reads our book, he'll know that we did follow his clue.

"Maybe, we shouldn't tell our readers what Argus means, Nana. If they're curious they can look it up for themselves."

"Adam we don't want to irritate our readers. If most of our readers are tourists they just want to have fun on their vacations. I think it is a terrific name and it proves the experts thought of every little detail, and never missed an opportunity to make history exciting. Don't you think that Argus is a good name for a history navigator?"

"Yes," agreed Adam. "Since it watches you and guards the library. But Nana I never thought the history of the HC could be this exciting either."

"Speaking of names, Mr. Knight also told me how LAWSON'S LANDING RIVERWALK CAFÉ got it's name."

"Don't tell me," said Adam. "I know you're going to say it was named by a committee."

"In a way," she answered. "But, since the café is inside the HC this time the committee also asked the public for suggestions. There were no rules, the name didn't have to mean anything, and they received hundreds of suggestions.

"The committee kept narrowing the names down and the list got smaller and smaller until they had five, then they asked the TP staff to select their three favorite ones. Then, when they signed the café concession with a vendor, they gave the vendor the top two names and the vendor picked the winning name.

"It seems to me then, that pretty much everyone we see working at the HC has been involved in a committee, in one way or another.

"They also needed to make money to run the HC, Adam. I know you'll be as glad to learn that all of the money from ticket and museum store sales stays right here to support education programs and to preserve TPC's historic collections, buildings, and gardens.

"They also developed other ways to earn money by renting classrooms, Mattocks Hall, the Cullman Performance Hall, and other HC areas to the public for different sorts of meetings and events, like a wedding.

Looking over her notes, Nana said "Oh, Adam, Mr. Knight said he knew the Frosts. I know that you remember the story I told you about Gavin and Yvonne Frost being real witches."

"Nana, I'll never forget that story."

"Well, Mr. Knight said that he met the witches when he moved here and bought his house because they were his backyard neighbors.

"I told him I knew the witches, but I didn't tell him the stories about your mom or Uncle Joel."

"Nana, maybe he'll be surprised if he reads our book."

"Maybe," she said. "Maybe some of the stories in our book will surprise a lot of people.

"It looks like there's a couple of classes from Pitt County schools having lunch on the patio, maybe we could arrange for your class to make a field trip here, like when all of the third graders at your school went on a field trip to visit Raleigh's Lost Colony."

"Maybe, but I want to see it before I recommend it to my class Nana."

"Well, after hearing about the history of the HC I thought you would recommend coming here just so they can see what a brain-storming committee of determined people with big ideas can accomplish," she replied.

"Yea, I can recommend the history part of the HC, Nana, but I would rather go through the time portals before I recommend the time traveling museum part."

"I'm glad you won't recommend something until you've tried it, so I understand Adam.

"Are you ready to go time traveling?"

This Might Be Adam's Tipping Point

"Time traveling in our new HC was a very different and exciting experience than you might find in a traditional museum, Adam. Did you enjoy it?"

"I loved it Nana, but don't you want to go to the museum store now?"

"Yes and you can buy a souvenir."

Pointing to a display obviously filled with items that children might want, Adam suggested, "Let's start here, Nana I want to look at that Irish Penny Whistle."

After spending several minutes looking around, Adam started playing with a Jacob's Ladder toy, examining it.

Holding up the colorful string of blocks, while turning the top block back and forth so that the blocks tumbled down one after the other, he said, "Nana, I can see how this works, look how the ribbons let the blocks unfold."

"That is interesting Adam but let's go to that section where all of the books are. I cannot help but wonder if our book will ever be for sale here. Do you think it will?"

"I hope so Nana, because I don't see any children's history adventure books for sale."

"Adam, I know that you remember the reason we wanted to go on an adventure into the history of your hometown was so that we could write a book about it and hopefully make enough money so when the time comes you can send yourself to school."

"And to college, Nana."

"And to college," Nana repeated. "And universities, I am hoping you continue your education until you have a least one doctorate.

"We're all proud of you for being in academically gifted classes and for earning other academic recognitions, because one of the most important things we've learned from you adventure into history is the importance of an education.

"I'm also glad you got to hear the story about the history of the HC so that you can see how doing your best and thinking big can create tipping points for good things to happen.

"In researching history, and even in everyday life, you want to be on the lookout for important moments known as tipping-points. I know that when you think about it you'll understand that tipping-points are important because they can change everything.

"Our Baron wrote about his dozen misfortunes, Adam, but it was the Tuscarora Indian War that was our Baron's tipping-point, because it almost wiped New Bern off the map and ended his American adventure.

"I mention tipping-points because that's what I think the HC is for New Bern. Now, 300 years later, New Bern, NC can rival Williamsburg, VA as the first destination tourists choose when they want to experience America's colonial history, after all America's and Carolina's history began around your hometown.

"I know why we love New Bern, but I wanted to find out the top three reasons visitors fall in love with your hometown and want to move to New Bern.

"I explained to Pat Gulley and Cindi Lou DeVoe, they both work at the HC, that New Bern has benefited from so many talented people relocating here and I was interested in knowing their top 3 reasons they moved to New Bern.

"Ms. Gulley said she and her husband moved here from Chicago, Illinois, almost 20 years ago when he accepted a job offer. They accepted the offer because they love the milder weather, but still with all four seasons; the excellent medical facilities close by; and because New Bern is safe and charming, they enjoy wandering around downtown; and they love how easy it is to get to the rivers, and to the beach.

Ms. DeVoe said that she moved here from Ohio about 16 years ago because she thinks New Bern is 'a water paradise'. She loves the weather and the fact that New Bern is a river town and near ocean beaches and that it's historic, because she loves history, she's even been on the trolley tour through the historic district.

"Last week, I met a couple having lunch at Lawson's café; the Livingstons said they decided to move here three weeks after sailing into port. Mr. Livingston said he liked New Bern because the people who live here are so friendly. She said that when they were getting ready to sail away she did not want to leave and she hugged the pier's post because she did not want him to untie the rope securing their sailboat.

Then Ms. Livingston said, 'You want to know the top three reasons I moved to New Bern? It's because I love it! I love it! I love it!'

"They explained that they loved New Bern because it's so charming and it's so interesting living around here, because you can go day-tripping to so many different kinds of places. They really enjoy going to the outer banks and riding the ferries."

"Me too, Nana, I loved riding the ferry and going to the outer banks."

"So did I," Nana replied, adding, "And like us, they loved to roam around downtown and said they can understand why Middle Street was on the '10 Best Downtown Streets in the Country' list, or maybe it was the '10 Prettiest Downtown Streets in the Country' list, but we all agreed that both statements were true regardless of any list.

"But really Adam, you can't just pick-out one street. You can't leave out Pollock Street or Metcalf Street or East Front Street or Craven Street or Broad Street or any of the other streets in the historical district, because it's all of them together that makes your hometown so charming.

Opening the cover of a book, Nana said, "Look at this book Adam, *A New Bern Album* by John B. Green III, published 1985 by Tryon Palace Commission in New Bern. Do you remember Mr. Green?"

"Yes. Mr. Green works at the library and he picked out a book for me when I asked him what book he recommended for the following in our Baron's footsteps part of my adventure. I'll never forget how surprised I was when I got home and found a copy of our Baron's map of New Bern glued inside.

"No wonder people fall in love with your hometown Adam, these old pictures in Mr. Green's book really shows off New Bern's charm. For my souvenir I'm going to buy his book, what are you going to buy?"

"I really would like to learn how to play that Irish Penny Whistle."

The Ending

"We've never written a book before Adam, yet, by some miracle, here we are writing the last chapter. This is the part where we'll tell about having lunch at Lawson's Landing Riverwalk Café and when we went to the museum galleries at the HC, but we still haven't explored the outside of the HC yet.

"Since you're out of school for Spring Break, let's go back to the HC. I mean right now. It's 7:00a.m., and hardly anyone will be around this early, so it's the perfect time to get some exercise roaming around downtown and exploring around the HC. We can pretend we're tourists and take the rest of the pictures we need for our book and to post on your adventure into history website.

"I'd like to take another picture of you in front of the bust of our Baron's relative. I took that first picture of you beside the bust when you were five years old and, you know, when you believed it was really our Baron. I would like to take another picture now, when you're nine years old and you know the truth."

As before, Adam was sitting on the curb in front of the bust when he asked, "Nana do you think we're the only ones who knows this is really a bust of our Baron's relative?"

"No, I'm sure we're not the only ones to read about it on Ms. de Graffenried's website.

"Let's go to the HC Adam, we're finished taking pictures downtown; and after we finish taking our outside pictures at the HC, we'll have breakfast at Lawson's café and try to finish writing our book.

"Wait a minute; I don't want to forget to take a picture of one of the parking lot signs that are here to remind visitors that the HC is green. By-the-way, Adam, when I was reading the information on GreenCraven.org's website, I noticed they recognized The Epiphany School, that Nicolas Sparks and his associates founded, was also a green organization."

Crossing Cannon Gateway, they turned left and Nana took pictures of Adam as they explored the piers and a replica of a ship where children could play, before continuing to the patio's side entrance to the cafe.

Suddenly, Nana said, "Adam, stop! I can see us in the window. Let's take a picture of our reflection in the HC window. Can you see us?"

"Yes!" he replied. "Let me see the picture on the camera. I like it Nana, it looks like we're inside looking outside and I can see what's behind us, too, and because it's just our refection, Nana, it's not really us!"

Settling down at their table, Nana took a sheet of paper out of her pocket, saying "Adam, to finish our chapter on the history of the HC I want to tell you about an email I sent to Trish Ashburn, she's the Marketing and Communications Manager for Tryon Palace (TP). She also requested some information about your book and I sent her the text of one of the shorter chapters.

"I told you that TP has seven curators and I know that because Ms. Ashburn listed them for us in her reply. I want to read to you a little of what she wrote:

Hi Charlotte,

Adam's Adventure sounds wonderful!

For curators, we have the following:

Karen Ipock—Curator of Education

Brandon Anderson—Curator of Interpretation

Dean Knight—Curator for Collections Research and Interpretation

Rose McMahon—Curator of Exhibitions

Penne Sandbeck—Curator for Education research and Interpretation

Peter Sandbeck—Curator of Architecture

Lisa Wimpfheimer—Curator of Gardens

She also said that they anticipate 147,000 visitors to the Palace by the end of June, and since the HC, opened palace attendance has increased about 40%. Then I saw on the news that they had almost 180,000 visitors this year

"Nana, did she really say that she thought my adventure 'sounds wonderful'?"

"She really did, Adam, and I think she meant it and she also wished us good luck, but what do you think about all of the different curators, don't you think that their titles are interesting?

"I didn't know TP had curators, Nana, because I never thought about it before, but I'm glad to know about curators and how a museum's exhibits tell stories.

"Now, whenever I go to a museum I'll know the curators picked everything out for a reason and I'll try to figure out what it's saying, it will be like solving a history mystery."

"And I know that you like solving mysteries and when you understand the goal of an exhibit it certainly will make museums more interesting than they already are.

Well, Adam, that finishes the HC chapter.

"I guess you could sum it all up by saying that the TPC's team took on an important challenge to clean-up an embarrassing mess and built something we all can be proud of."

"Nana I think we should say that they turned an embarrassing mess into perfection, because the HC did turnout to be perfect."

"That does sound better Adam, but to finish the book don't you think we should write something about what you did on your adventure to the HC?"

"No, Nana, I don't think we should spoil the surprise for people who haven't been to the HC yet. Don't you think that would be like someone telling you the surprise ending of a book you're reading? That happened to me when I was reading my first Harry Potter book and believe me Nana I did not like it at all!"

"Well, you do have a good point Adam, but we have to say something. How about this, what if we tell about what parts we liked the most? My favorite part was getting lost in the storm."

"Nana, we got lost in the storm because you kept shouting 'Go south-east! Go south-east!'"

"Adam, you do have to agree it was hard to stay calm in a storm like that."

"It wasn't as hard as when I was the chef and I had to whack 200 rats!"

"I could hardly believe they had whacking rats as an interactive exhibit, but it was probably a realistic part of ship life.

"But now it's your turn Adam, what was your favorite part?"

"The Pepsi Family Center," Adam replied, steadfastly refusing to answer any more questions, or to elaborate any further, except to say "The End!"

PART 2: ADAM'S BORING (but interesting to Nana) DETAILS SECTION

Imagine You Are An Explorer

"Adam, can you imagine what the Indians must have thought when they saw England's first explorers. I wanted to know what happened so I went online to The National Archives of the United Kingdom. I requested permission to modernize some reports I found because they are in the difficult to read Elizabethan style.

"The reports had been written by three of the explores sent here by Sir Walter Raleigh telling him what happened when they came here and after you read them you'll understand why I wanted to include them in our book."

"And probably why they're in the boring section," retorted Adam, but with an approving smile, adding, "but don't worry Nana, I know that someday I'll want to read the boring part."

"Well I hope you do, someday, and I want to let you know that when I'm writing the boring part I'm pretending that you haven't banished them yet, and when I write something that you said it will be the truth because it will be something you really said earlier when we discussed the matter. Okay?"

"Okay, Nana."

"Imagine you're an explorer: Captain Arthur Barlowe, Sir Walter Raleigh personally came to give you his instructions before sending you into history. Raleigh and his friends have spent plenty of money on this mission, and even the Queen of England has high expectations for your success. Failure was not an option even though the mission was to travel into the unknown world, and full of danger.

"That first voyage is a reconnaissance expedition to a wild and wonderful continent in the New World, sent to claim the land and to collect information needed to establish Raleigh's first colony. Upon your return, you write a report for Raleigh; something like my modernized version of the original reports, housed in the Historical Collection, of the University of North Carolina at Chapel Hill, Wilson Library, Old South Leaflets No. 92.

THE FIRST VOYAGE TO ROANOKE, 1584

THE FIRST VOYAGE MADE TO THE COASTS OF AMERICA, WITH TWO BARKS, WHEREIN WERE CAPTAINS M. PHILIP AMADAS, AND M. ARTHUR BARLOWE, WHO DISCOVERED PART OF THE COUNTREY NOW CALLED VIRGINIA ANNO 1584. WRITTEN BY ONE OF THE SAID CAPTAINES, AND SENT TO SIR WALTER RALEGH, KNIGHT, AT WHOSE CHARGE AND DIRECTION, THE SAID VOYAGE WAS SET FORTH.

MAY GOD BE WITH US AS HE WAS WITH OUR FOREFATHERS

April 27, 1584 we departed the west of England, with two barks well furnished with men, and foods, having received our last and perfect directions by your letters, confirming the former instructions, and commandments delivered by yourself at our leaving the river of Thames. Thinking it would be tedious and not necessary to remember all of that or the sailing back and forth, so beginning with our main discovery of your Country, now called Virginia. Presented here is a brief report, which might help prove it a profitable success for you and to her Highness, and the Commonwealth. We performed our services at your direction and we hope you are satisfied with your decision considering we learned much more than we expected or hoped.

The tenth of May we arrived at the Canaries and the Islands of the West Indies on tenth of June, where we got fresh water and food; we sailed so far south because we thought the current from the Bay of Mexico between the Cape of Florida and Havana would be greater than it was.

July 2, 1584 the air brings a sweet smell so strong that you would think you were in the best garden smelling the perfume of many different kinds of flowers and begin to see shoal water; calling all hands to be on watch as land is near. July 4[th,] we arrived upon the coast, which we supposed to be a continent.

First, we thanked God for our safe voyage, and then we rowed to the sandy beach. We went through the proper procedure and ceremony, planted the flag of England, and claimed the land in the name of her Majesty Queen Elizabeth and for Sir Walter Raleigh, then climbing the sandy hills we discovered another great sea on the other side and a mainland, and realized we were on an island.

The string of islands runs for two hundred miles, we sailed along the outer banks, blocked from crossing through by dangerous shallows. Ships are in constant peril of shipwreck all along these barrier islands and all hands watched for dangerous sand bars. After trying many places, for a hundred and twenty miles we finally get our ships through with the help of the tide. We drop anchor and had been sitting beside this Island for two days before we saw any people. When we shot our guns great flocks of birds would rise up making as great a noise as if a whole army were shouting altogether.

On the third day, we saw a small boat with three people in it. The boat landed and two stayed with the boat, but the other one walked towards us and reaching the point of land next to us, he then walked up and down the point making gestures for us to come ashore. Bringing the pilot, Simon Ferdinando, Captain Amadas, and some others we rowed to the bank where he stood. The fellow, never showing any fear, began to speak but we could not understand him.

After awhile, when the fellow was finished talking we gestured in a sort of sign language if he wanted to come aboard our ships and understanding our invitation he joyfully accepted.

Amazed at our clothes, he being dress only in a deerskin, we suffered him touching us. We gave him a shirt and a hat and showed him some of the merchandise we had and gave him some of the trinkets he liked, before he left we offered him wine and meat to eat which he liked very much.

Then after seeing both our barks, he left the ship and getting his own boat, went into the water for a little way, and started fishing. We watched as he filled his boat in less than a half-hour, as full as it could be with out sinking. Then he came back to the point of land, and divided his fish into two parts, then pointing from the piles of fish towards our ships, indicating a pile of fish for each as if he, in his own way, was trying to repay us for the gifts given him. Then they left.

The next day many boats, with forty or fifty men came; in one is the King's brother Granganimeo. He does as the first man did and when he walked along the same point of land near our ships followed by forty of his men, the rest being servants who laid a very large mat upon the ground; where he sat at one end and four of his companions sat at the other end. The rest of his men stood round behind them, but not very close.

Even though we had our weapons none of them moved or showed any fear, or mistrust of us, that we might harm them.

Then, smiling, he made welcoming gestures to come and

sit by him. When we did so he commenced to making all sorts of joyful signs of welcome, striking with his hand both his head and his breast and then doing the same on our head and breast, showing we should be friends and trying, as best he could, to show us love.

No one interrupted him or even spoke the whole time, except from time to time when one of the four would whisper very softly to the other three.

After he had made a long speech, we could not understand we gave him presents, making him very happy, giving us many thanks for our gifts.

After we gave to the king's brother the presents we thought he would like we then gave presents to the four who sat at the other end of the mat. After a moment, Granganimeo went to each and took everything we had given them putting them into his own basket and making signs and gestures that all things belonged to him as the others were his followers and servants.

The King is always obeyed and he and his brothers and children are revered. They are very handsome and goodly people, and in their behavior as mannerly and civil as any of Europe. You know from the two Indians we brought back that no other people in the world show more respect for their governing nobility than these people.

Their chief Lord, Wingina, we did not see as he was at their main town, six days away. He was recuperating from wounds received in a recent fight with neighboring kingdoms. Wingina had two serious wounds in his body, and another very serious wound caused by an arrow going all of the way through his thigh. These people are constantly at war with the adjoining kingdoms; which is so deadly it keeps the tribe's populations from increasing and some areas have become desolated, the inhabitants wiped out.

A day or two later they came back with deerskins and chamois buffs and we began trading, he especially liked a shinny tin dish. He punched a hole in the rim and hung it around his neck on a string, making signs that it would protect him from the arrows of his enemies.

We traded the tin dish for twenty deerskins, worth twenty Crowns, or twenty Nobles: and we traded a copper kettle for fifty skins worth fifty Crowns.

We were happy with the trades for our axes, hatches, knives and although they offered us anything we wanted for our swords, we would not trade our swords.

Two or three days later Granganimeo came aboard and we fed him wine and meat that he thought was very good.

After several more days had passed he brought his wife who is very bashful, and two or three of his children. His wife is handsome and average size. She wore a cape of leather down her back with the fur inside and another piece in front like an apron.

Around her head, she wore a wreath of white Coral, and so did her husband. Many long bracelets hung from her ears down to her middle, and from around her neck, all made of pearls as large as the biggest peas, like the pearl bracelet given to your worship, as did some of Granganimeo's children. Other noble men and women had five or six copper pendants hanging from their ears. They decorate their bodies with bracelets tattooed around their legs, arms, and neck.

Granganimeo wore a wide metal plate on his head made of gold or copper, not being polished we could not tell. He would not allow it to be removed, but did allow us to touch it, we discovered it was not ridged, but it could be bowed. He dresses like his wives, but men wear their hair differently. Women wear their hair shoulder length and soft hanging down on both sides. However, the men wind up their hair on each side, into a knot behind each ear; using a feather, a bone, or some other thing to hold it in place. And from the forehead down the center of his head runs a long row of hair shaped like a cock's comb but ends in a long tail hanging down the middle of his back, but sometimes it is rolled up into a knot at the nape of his neck. Their skin is tinged yellow and the adults have blackish color hair but some children had chestnut or auburn color hair.

After the nobles were finished trading, a great number of people came on board, bringing dressed skins and coral and many other very nice things to trade but if Granganimeo was there no one but the nobles with red copper on their heads dared to come aboard to trade with us.

The wife of the king's brother came to our ship many times and always brought two daughters and a couple of nurses on board, leaving forty or fifty more women waiting on the shore.

Whenever Granganimeo came, he always had the same number of fires lit on a far away shore as he had boats before they got to close to the ship. He did this in order to show us how many boats were with him so we would not be surprised.

They have no metal edged tools. About twenty years earlier, they found nails and spikes among the few pieces of the demolished remains of a ship, cherishing them as their best tools, but do not know how to make them.

They make their boats from one pitch Pine tree. They burn down a great tree by setting fire around the tree's base until it falls down, or when they find one the wind has knocked down. To down a tree or to hollow out the hole they cover the area with gummy rosin and set it on fire scraping the burnt wood with shells and repeating this until it is the way they want it, making very fine boats that can hold twenty men plus baggage. To navigate, depending on how deep the water, they use long poles or wooden oars shaped like a large scoop.

Granganimeo greatly admired our suits of armor and wanted to trade a huge box of pearls for a suite of armor, a sword, and a few other things, but this time we refused because we did not want him to know how much we wanted his pearls before we found out where he got them. Your worship now understands why.

He was very honest and never failed to bring the items he promised and he brought us the best food in the world everyday: a couple of fat deer, coons, rabbits, all kinds of fresh fish, all kinds of fresh roots and fruits, white maize, of which they harvest three crops in five months. They also brought melons, walnuts, cucumbers, gourds, peas, and beans.

After they had visited us many times I selected seven men to come with me to explore, going twenty miles into the river they call Occam.

Arriving the next evening at Roanoke Island, we anchored a little way distant from the natural harbor near the North end where there was a village of nine houses, built of Cedar, and fortified round about with sharp trees, to keep out their enemies.

As we got closer, the wife of Granganimeo ran to meet us appearing very happy to see us sending her servants to pull our boat ashore and to carry us on their backs to dry ground. She also ordered our oars brought so we would know they were safe.

Her husband was not at home but she and her servants brought us to her house, with five rooms. She ordered all of the arrangements for our comfort and quickly prepared a meal for us to eat.

Seating us around a great fire, she had her servants wash

and dry our clothes. Some of the women removed our shoes and stocking and washed them, some using warm water washed our feet. After we were dried and dressed she took us to another room, where she had a banquet set upon a long board; laden with roasted and boiled deer and fish, melons, roots and fruits of many different kinds of good food. We could chose our drinks of water as some being flavored with ginger, black cinnamon, sassafras, or other medicinal herbs, or grape wine.

She did her utmost to be gentle, loving, and kind and we found them to be free of treachery and guile and seemed to be living in the golden age of faithfulness.

Their land is so abundant and fruitful that their only need is to protect themselves from the cold during their brief winters. They cook very savory meats in large earthen pots and they eat off sweet wooden plates.

When we were eating, two or three men returned from hunting with their bows and arrows and when we saw them, we reached for our weapons, looking at one another.

When she saw us reach for our weapons and our look of mistrust she immediately had some of her men take the men's bows and arrows and breaking them over the poor fellow's heads and bodies, beating them all of the way out of the village.

As we were leaving, she was sorry we would not stay the night in her house and prepared a supper in pots for us to take. We moved our boat from the shore a little way where we stayed all night. It started raining and she came to the shore inviting us repeatedly to stay in their houses. She was very sorry because she could see our concerns on our faces. However, we were afraid, being so few and our mission so important, to take any chances. Even though we had nothing to fear from them, being the kindest, most generous and loving people in the whole world.

They said that twenty-six years ago a ship wrecked near their town of Secotan on the uninhabited island. The Indians found them ten days later. The Indians helped them lash two Indian boats together, made masts for it and a sail out of the sailor's shirts. The Indians gave them much food and after about three weeks, they were ready to cast off. Soon after the Indians found the two boats wrecked on another island but no one ever saw the people again. Since then they never saw any one with clothes or skin like ours until we arrived.

Besides marveling at our ships, they had admiration for everything we had, not ever having seen anything like them in all of their lives.

When we shot even our smallest gun they trembled in fear and awe; since they only had for weapons arrows made from cane reeds tipped with a bone or a fish tooth at one end, still it could kill a naked man, or an animal. They use wooden swords and wooden breastplates, the wood being hardened in the fire. They have flat wooden clubs with sharp deer horns or other sharp objects fastened at one end.

When they go to war, they take an idol of their God with them and ask it for guidance. Instead of drums, they sing as they march to war.

Beside this kingdom, Secotan, belonging to King Wingina, there is an adjoining kingdom, Pamlico, belonging to a King called Piemacum. This kingdom is in league with another kingdom the Secotan call Neusiok. Neusiok means 'the people of the Neuse', being a combination of Neuse, the Secotan's name for the river where their village is, and 'ok' meaning people. Theses savages are part of another larger kingdom that includes the town of two kings who are always at war with King Wingina. Even though towns and villages are not ten miles apart, they all speak different languages, causing great distrust and jealousies.

Two years earlier King Piemacum, under the pretext of making peace and friendship, invited the best people of Secotan to his town for a feast.

"When the men and thirty women, and their children were making merry and praying before their idol the Captain of the town and his men attacked the Secotan killing all of the men and enslaving the thirty women and all their children.

The two Indians we brought with us told this to us. Wingina asked us to go with them on a surprise attack of King Piemacum's town. Telling us we would find a great deal of merchandise and food, but we could not tell if it was because they loved us or because they wanted revenge and to free their relatives.

Beyond Roanoke Island, the mainland has many fruits and all kinds of plenty. There are many towns and villages along the side of the continent and stretching up into the land along the rivers and creeks.

When we first arrived, we thought that the islands were the country but when we got through, we saw that there was a great sea between them and the continent, There lies between the ocean and the mainland a track of islands two hundred miles long with only two or three entrances to pass through to the other side. These islands are very narrow, six miles broad, more in some places and less in other places.

When you pass through you are in a great-enclosed sea, some places twenty, forty, and fifty miles across to the mainland. There are at least a hundred islands of different sizes, one being sixteen miles long, which has the most pleasant and fertile land of any in the world. Besides this island, many others are two, three, four, or five miles long. They are very pleasant and beautiful to look at. Most are filled with and abundance of deer, bears, coons, rabbits, and many other different animals and the best fish and fowl in the world, all around them. The banks are sandy and low toward the waters side, but so full of scuppernong grapes they even over flow into the sea the waves washing over them. Grapes are so thick, everywhere, both on the sand and on the green soil on the hills, and in the plains, as well on every little shrub, and also climbing towards the tops of high cedars. It being so incredible to see, that such like abundance nowhere else found in the world. There are many other sweet woods, flax, sea oats, and many other wonderful things we did not have time to investigate.

Sir, with this report to record our discoveries on this reconnaissance voyage you will understand why we decided to come back to England so soon, to bring you the good news, and to let you know that we took possession of this great country for our Majesty and by her Majesty's grant for you.

Therefore, it is important to name the gentlemen and men who witnessed our discoveries and were present when we claimed the country for her Majesty's and on your behalf. Therefore, to prevent any doubts, or pretenders, they are here named: Master Arthur Barlowe, Captain; Master Philip Amadas, Captain; William Greenvile, John Wood, James Browewich, Henry Greene, Benjamin Wood, Simon Ferdinando, Nicholas Petman, John Hewes, of the company; and many others in our company I will not trouble you with the remembrance of their names.

Arriving safely, September 15, 1584, we brought home with us two of the Savages, vigorous healthy men, whose names are Wanchese and Manteo.

"That's the end of Barlowe's report, isn't it amazing Adam, right then and right there they planted the flag of England on July 4, 1584 on Carolina's Crystal Coast, of course, back then, it was still Virginia's coast, Carolina would not be carved out of Virginia for 79 more years.

"You mean that North Carolina use to be Virginia?" asked Adam.

"Not only North Carolina but other states were carved out of Virginia as well. Virginia was huge, and it included all of America not previously claimed by another country, all the way to the islands in the oceans. We will not go into that because you will learn all about it in school.

"It's important to follow a timeline if you want to see how one thing leads to the next. If you just jump around from time to time and from one event to another things are out of context and can often be deceiving.

"One of the interesting things about research is that we are in their world and time and we can see how things develop but we know what is going to happen in the future.

"That first meeting between the Old and the New Worlds in Virginia seems to have been a positive experience with a good ending and the report is important to us because that's the first time that the Neuse River and the Neusiok Indians who lived here are written about. What do you think Adam?"

Adam, thoughtful for a moment before declaring, "I'm glad that Sir Walter Raleigh's explorers knew how to write and I think that he has to send another expedition. They can't take Manteo and Wanchese to England and not bring them back home Nana, that would be kidnapping.

Imagine You Are An Indian

"Imagine you are an Indian from a little village with 9 huts and if you added together all the other villages of your tribe there would only be about 700 warriors and your limited vocabulary doesn't have the words to express the wonders you will see in the Old World.

"You have just landed in England and soon will meet the Queen of England and Walter Raleigh. Nothing in your life has prepared you for England though, when you arrive, September 15, 1584.

"Adam, there were 50,000 people living in London back then. Compare that to the 2010 census that says New Bern's population is only 29,524.

"Manteo and Wanchese don't see their familiar world of canoes on the river, or huts built of reeds and sticks lining the shore, or animal paths to travel upon, or people dressed in deerskins.

"For the first time, Wanchese and Manteo see great docks with hundreds of tall ships, and all kinds of other ships and boats, and huge bales of merchandise coming ashore that came from all over a world they never before knew existed.

"People are dressed in fabulous clothes made from silk, wool, and linen. Amazing sights are everywhere, including: life-size statues; musical instruments; people riding on the backs of animals; wagons and carriages with wheels are rolling along; pulled by strange animals like oxen, donkeys, and horses; great churches with bells; castles, and palaces with hundreds of rooms, and houses with beautiful landscaped lawns and gardens.

"There's a whirlwind of activity all around Raleigh and it seems all of London wants to see the 'Savages' brought back by Raleigh's men.

"Raleigh presents you to the Queen; at a palace with furniture and furnishings, and pomp and ceremony, which will be impossible for you to describe when you return home.

Pausing for a moment, as if to let the picture sink into Adam's imagination, Nana asked, "Adam can we really imagine what it was like for Manteo and Wanchese to go from Roanoke to England in 1584?

"They had never before seen wheels, or horses. There were no horses, or cows, or sheep in the New World, that is until the explorers and settlers brought them here. Seeing people riding on a horse's back for the first time Indians thought it was an animal that was half- animal and half- man."

Surprised, Adam wanted to make sure she meant what he though she had said and asked, "You mean they really thought it had the body of a horse and the head and arms of a man?"

"Yes," replied Nana. "Not only that, when they learned the truth they were equally amazed that an animal would allow a man to ride on it's back.

"The explorers on the first voyage were only here for six or seven weeks but they learned enough of the Indian's vocabulary that they could communicate a little even then; plus, Manteo and Wanchese learned even more English on the way to England so they could talk to Raleigh and the Queen. England's royal website, http://www.royal.gov.uk, explains it all and even said Queen Elizabeth I could speak six languages, so I suspect she was probably interested in their language and enjoyed talking to them.

"Raleigh was pleased that the first expedition went so well and was very profitable earning a thousand percent on the goods they brought back to England, which was mostly furs."

"It's told how the Queen graciously accepted the very first pipe of tobacco, after Raleigh lit it and showed her how to smoke. Inhaling a whiff of the smoke, she began coughing so violently and felt sick to her stomach that Raleigh's enemies whispered around court that Raleigh was trying to poison the Queen.

"Hearing the rumors and felling better, the Queen insisted that the Countess of Nottingham and her ladies in waiting all share a whole pipe full; when none of them died that ended those rumors.

"Manteo and Wanchese had been in England for almost a year when they left on August 17, 1585 to go back to Roanoke."

"I can imagine that the people on Roanoke Island are wondering what happened to Manteo and Wanchese, since they have been gone so long," mentioned Adam.

"And I can imagine that the Queen and Raleigh were eager to read the reports from Captain Barlowe, Ralph Lane and John White," chimed in Nana.

"I'm glad he sends John White this time so that we can still see what the Indians looked like Nana, and I would be happy if I was Raleigh, after reading Captain Barlowe's report," Adam decided, "because the Indians were friendly and nice and wanted to trade with them."

"Raleigh must have thought the same way, Adam, because he decides to plant his first colony in the new world on Roanoke Island.

"This second voyage can cause confusion if you do not remember that the first voyage was only an exploration mission to find the best place to settle a colony. Even though he started working right away, it took a whole year of planning for settling the first colony before everything was ready.

"Adam, the definition of colony is a group of people who leave their native country to settle a new land that has ties to their native 'Mother' country. The new land is Virginia and Raleigh's colony, the 'City of Raleigh', is Virginia's first real estate subdivision.

"Adam, since the privateers share the plunder taken from the Spanish ships with the Queen, pirating is more respectable and the Queen's best adventurers were privateers, including, Raleigh, and Sir Frances Drake. Not only was Raleigh founding a colony but they choose Roanoke Island for other good reasons, the main one being that it's hidden behind the outer banks since it was also going to be their hideout base, after their pirating raids on Spanish ships. It was also the perfect location for a base for English ships during the war they knew was coming with Spain.

"Adam, remember everything that has already happened. Wingina's father, Ensinore, and his brother, King Granganimeo both believe Barlowe and his men are their dead ancestors, heaven sent by God from Skyland to help them.

"Now they're expecting Manteo and Wanchese to return with a report of England, the Queen, and Raleigh."

"Nana, I think they asked Manteo and Wanchese if they thought that England was Heaven. I think Manteo and Wanchese might believe England was Heaven because it was so different, Nana."

"You're probably correct, Adam. However, what they saw in England turns Wanchese into an enemy, but Manteo remained a friend. I think most of the Indians were probably confused because Wanchese and Manteo did not have the words to tell their tribes about the wonders they saw, because everything was so strange and different from anything they had ever experienced, it was impossible for the Indians to imagine the truth about the rest of the world.

"Adam, in Barlowe's report he tells how he refused to help Wingina destroy his enemies. We can only imagine how Wingina and the other Indians must have felt when they tried to understand what was going on and now, here the Gods are back, again, but this time with a lot more ships and over a hundred men with swords and guns will be staying after the ships leave.

"Now, company is one thing, Adam, but when that means you have hundreds of extra mouths to feed, for God knows how long, after awhile it must have seemed a great burden to Wingina and his followers. Grenville left 108 settlers and that's a lot of people to feed even for one meal."

"Yeah," agreed Adam, "I think they're lucky Lord Wingina treated them as friends and fed them everyday," decided Adam.

"I think they are lucky too," said Nana. "I've already told you about Captain Barlowe's report, which of course you didn't read because you've banished it, and the next two are also from England's National Archives that are housed at the University of NC at Chapel Hill."

"Hurry and get to that part, Nana, I want to hear what they saw, but I still might banish them."

"Okay. I was just reminding you that I'm trying to modernize real reports by using words that we might use today so they will be easier to understand."

Then, handing him a calculator Nana asked "Adam, if you subtract 1585 from 2011 what is the answer?"

"426, Nana that means they wrote the reports 426 years ago. It really is dead men talking."

Imagine You Are An Artist

A Brief And True Report Of The New Found Land Of Virginia

"Imagine that you are John White, Esquire, surveyor, and a talented artist, handpicked and sent by Raleigh to illustrate what you see and write about what happened on your adventure to the New World.

"This next part is just a few of the descriptions that are included in the report: from the electronic edition of the UNC-CH digitization project, Documenting the American South and housed at the University of North Carolina at Chapel Hill: Call number VC 970.1 H23b (North Carolina Collection, University of North Carolina at Chapel Hill). Adam, our readers can read the entire original reports and see John White's watercolors online at the website: http://docsouth. unc.edu/nc/hariot/hariot.html.

A Brief and True Report of the New Found Land of Virginia: of the Commodities and of the Nature and Manners of the Natural Inhabitants: Discovered by the English Colony there, seated by Sir Richard Grenville, Knight, in the year 1585: which remained under the Government of twelve months, at the special charge and direction of the Honourable Sir Walter Raleigh, Knight Lord Warden of the Stannaries, who therein has been favored and authorized by Her Majesty and Her Letters Patents / This book is written in English by Thomas Hariot sergeant to the above-named Sir Walter, a member of the colony, and there employed in discovering;...

THE TRUE PICTURES AND FASHIONS OF
THE PEOPLE IN THAT PART
OF AMERICA NOW CALLED
VIRGINIA, DISCOVRED BY ENGLISMEN
sent there in the year of our Lord 1585. At the special charge
and direction of the Honourable Sir Walter Raleigh, Knight,
Lord Warden of the Stannaries in the duchies of Cornwall
and Oxford who has been favored and authorized by Her
Majesty and her Letters Patents.
Translated out of Latin into English by Richard HACKLVIT.
Diligently collected and drawn
by John White who was sent their speciallye and for the
same purpose
By the said Sir Walter Raleigh the year above said
1585. and also the year 1588. Now cut in copper and first
Published and paid for by THEODORE de BRY.

The Arrival Of The Englishmen In Virginia

The seacoasts of Virginia are full of Islands, so an entrance to get to the mainland is hard to find, a large division seems a convenient entrance, yet to our great peril, we proved that they are shallow, and full of dangerous flats.

We could never pierce open into the main land, until we made trials in many places with our small pinnaces; after our men's diligent search, we finally found our way through.

Not very long after we passed through we discovered a mighty river falling down into the sound, but could not sail up river because it was so shallow, the mouth being filled with sands driven in with the tide.

Sailing further, we came to a very large island. As soon as the Inhabitants saw us they began to make, a great and horrible cry, as if they had never before seen men attired like us. Coming to the shore, crying out like wild beasts or men out of their wits, then, running away as we got closer; but gently called back, we offered them our wares holding up: glasses, knives, baby dolls, and other trifles, which we thought would delight them. So they stood still, and perceiving our good will and courtesy came fawning upon us, and bade us welcome.

Then they brought us to their village on the island called Roanoke, which is very pleasant and has plenty of fish. Their Wiroans or Prince entertained us with reasonable courtesy although amazed at the first sight of us.

Such was our arrival into the part of the world, which we call Virginia.

My illustrations show the Princes of Virginia in their attire, now, I will describe for you, the people, their attire, and manner of living, their feasts, and banquets.

A Wiroan Or Great Lord Of Virginia

They wear the hair on their heads long and bind up the ends in a knot under their ears. Yet they cut the top of their heads from the forehead to the nape of the neck in manner of a cockscomb, sticking a fair large piece of some bird at the beginning of the crest upon their foreheads, and another short one on both sides about their ears.

Hanging from their ears is either large pearls, or something else, like the claw of some great bird, or something else they like.

They tattoo, or paint their forehead, cheeks, chin, body, arms, and legs but different from the inhabitants of Florida. They wear long chains about their necks of pearls or beads of copper, which they prize, and bracelets on their arms. Under their breasts about their bellies appear certain spots, used to bleed them, when they are sick.

They hang before them an apron from the skin of some beast very finely dressed in such away as the tail hangs down behind.

They carry a quiver made of small rushes holding their bow ready bent in on hand, and an arrow in the other, ready to defend themselves, in this manner they go to war, or to their solemn feasts and banquets.

They take much pleasure in hunting deer, there is great abundance in this country, for it is fruitful, pleasant, and full of goodly woods. There are also many rivers full of different kinds of fish.

When they go to battle, they paint their bodies in the most terrible manner that they can devise.

A Chief Lord Of Roanoke

All the chief men of the island and town of Roanoke raise the hair of their crowns of their heads cut like a cockscomb. The rest wear their hair up in a knot in the nape of their necks as women do.

They hang strings of pearls at their ears, and wear bracelets on their arms of pearls, or small beads of copper or a smooth bone called minsal.

They neither paint nor tattoo them selves, but in token of authority, and honor, they wear a chain of great pearls, or copper beads or smooth bones about their necks, and a long plate of copper hanging nearly to the middle of their thighs.

They cover themselves before and behind as the women do with a deer's skin handsomely dressed, and fringed, More over they fold their arms together as they walk, or as they talk one with another, it being to them a sign of wisdom.

About The Chief Ladies Of Secotan

The women of Secotan are well proportion. In their going they carry their hands dangling down, and are draped in a deerskin apron, excellently dressed, hanging down almost to the middle of their thighs, also covering their hinder parts. The rest of their bodies are all bare.

The front of their hair short the rest is not over long, thin, and soft, and falling down about their shoulders: They wear a wreath about their heads. Their foreheads, cheeks, chin, arms, and legs are tattooed. They wear a chain, around their necks either tattooed or painted.

They have small eyes, plain and flat noses, narrow foreheads, and broad mouths. Most have long chains of pearls hanging around their necks and from their ears, or of some smooth bones. Their nails are not long, as the women of Florida. They are also delighted with walking into the fields, and besides the rivers, to see the hunting of deer, and catching fish.

The Different Marks Of The Chief Men Of Virginia

The inhabitants of all the kingdoms for the most part have marks razed on their backs, whereby it may be known what Princes subjects they are, or of what place they have their origin. For which cause we have set down those marks in this drawing, and have listed the names of the places, in order that they might be easily recognized.

Although they seem to be very simple, and crude God has given them everything they need in abundance. To tell the truth, I cannot remember, ever seeing a better or quieter people than they.

Pausing, Nana asked, "Adam, I was just wandering if they made the marks on a baby's back right away, you know, when the baby was born?"

"I think they did, Nana. How else could they know if a baby belonged to their tribe when it was kidnapped, babies can't talk," reasoned Adam.

"That's not all White wrote, we can go online to read the rest of the descriptions and see his drawings of the marks and all of the other illustrations he made for Raleigh.

"I read this part of White's report first to set the stage and describe the Indians so we can better understand what happens next." Nana warned, "Real trouble starts in just three weeks."

They Ruin It For Everyone

"Sir Richard Grenville is in charge of the fleet of seven ships, carrying: 108 settlers, a lot of sailors, Manteo and Wanchese, smallpox and probably measles too.

"Adam, the Indians didn't know about science so when the Indians got sick and died from these new, strange diseases they thought they had been shot by invisible bullets that had been sent to kill them.

"This is the second time Raleigh has sent people here. First was a small group of explorers on a mission, to find the best location for Raleigh's first colony.

"Those in the second group are settlers sent to settle on Roanoke Island, Governor Ralph Lane assumes responsibility for the colony, Grenville explores, looking around, the sounds, and rivers, and visiting other Indian villages.

"One day, about three weeks after Grenville arrived he visited Aquascogoc, a village on the mainland, about where Pantego is now, near Bath, and invited the Indians to visit his ship.

"After the Indians left, he learned one of his silver cups was missing, believed stolen by one of the Indians. To teach the Indians a lesson Grenville ordered the total destruction of the village.

"Grenville, personally lead the attack. Not only did they tear down and set fire to all of the houses, but they also ruined their gardens, and killed the Indians including women and children. They said that they let a few run away so they would scare other Indians when they told them what happened to them at Aquascogoc.

"Now destroying their food and gardens is about as bad a killing them and this terrible news traveled fast and far. Where before the Indians had feared and loved them as Gods now they feared and hated them as Devils and refused to trade with them, or feed them.

"Refusing to feed them made the settlers hungry and angry and they started stealing the fish from the traps the Indians had built, sometimes even destroying the traps to steal the fish.

"All of this was going on, unknown to Lane who was on a reconnaissance mission to find the copper-mine and the pearl oyster beds.

"I can see poor Ralph Lane trying to write his report. He's disappointed and worried and he's probably pacing back and forth as he tries to find the right words to explain to Raleigh: what happened, what they did, what went wrong, and why they came back with Drake and without the pearls.

Imagine You Are Raleigh

Raleigh's First Roanoke Colony.

"You can look up this report about the second voyage to Roanoke Island, written by Ralph Lane, governor, using Call number Cp970.1 L26r (North Carolina Collection, University of North Carolina at Chapel Hill) Old South Leaflets No. 119, or you can see the illustrations and read the Electronic Edition online at http://docsouth.unc.edu/nc/lane/lane.html. "

An account by Ralph Lane sent and directed to Sir Walter Raleigh.

Of the particularities of the imployments of the English men left in Virginia by Sir Richard Grenville under the charge of Master Ralph Lane, General of the same, from August 17, 1585 until June18,1586 at which time they departed the Country;

This report is in two parts. The first relates our discoveries as our weak numbers and limited supply of things permitted. The second part, in the beginning tells about the conspiracy of Pemisapan, with the Savages on the mainland to cut us off and then the reasons we decided to leave with General Sir Francis Drake, when we lost the barks, pinnaces, and boats meant for us, the hurricane carrying all away.

The First Part: A Description Of Virginia

First, you shall understand that our discovery extends from the island of Roanoke, where we built Fort Raleigh and houses for the settlers, to the South, to the North, to the Northwest, and to the West. To the South we discovered the Secotan, being about 80 miles from Roanoke. The broad sound is full of flats and shoals, so only one of our boats with four oars could pass through and carry no more than fifteen men, with their furniture, baggage, and food for seven days at the most each time. As for our pinnace, besides that she needed a deeper water than that shallow sound, and other reasons plus winter was here, we thought it best to wait to explore the other areas until we were stronger supplied.

Northward our furthest discovery was to the Chesepians, about 130 miles from Roanoke, the way was very shallow and most dangerous because the sound was so broad there would be no help if we made a mistake.

Fifteen miles from the shore of the Chesepians is the most pleasant soil and temperature and the nearness to the sea, besides a multitude of bears, which are very good food and other good things, great woods of sassafras and walnut trees that there is no better place to be found.

While living there, all of the different kings of the

neighboring kingdoms came to visit our colony all with abundance of everything.

Then our discovery to the northwest was Chawanook, 130 miles is from Roanoke. Passage was through a broad, freshwater sound with a very good, deep navigable channel, but full of shoals outside of the channel. Where the river straightens and narrows is Weapomeiok, the kingdom of King Okisco. It is a very large town and the main town of this kingdom.

The towns about the waters situated by the way are these following Passaquenoke The woman's Town, Chepanoc, Weapomeiok, Muscamunge, & Metackwem: all these being under the jurisdiction of King Okisco. The river forks into two rivers from Muscamunge we enter into the bottom fork of the river, and jurisdiction of Chawanook: There the river begins to straighten until it come to Chawanook, and then becomes as narrow as the Thames between Westminster, and Lambeth, in England.

Between Muscamunge and Chawanook upon the left hand as we pass is good high land, and there is a Town, which we called the Blind Town, the inhabitants being blind, some in one eye, and some in both. The savages called it Ohanoak, and they have a very goodly maize-field: they are subject to Chawanook.

Chawanook itself is the greatest province lying upon that river, and it is able to put 700 fighting men into the field, in addition to the force of the province itself. Their King is called Menatonon, a man weak in his limbs, but otherwise for a savage, a very grave and wise man, and very good in matters concerning not only of his own kingdom and the disposition of his own men but also of his neighbors round about him, near or far, and of the commodities that each kingdom yields.

In March 1586, he was our prisoner, for the two days that we were together, he giving more understanding of the country than we learned from all our searches, or from any of the other savages

Among things, he told that going three days journey in a canoe, up Chawanook River, and then descending to the land, after four days journey over land northeast you reach a certain kingdom. This kingdom lies by the sea, but this king's place of greatest strength is an island, in a bay, the water round about the Island being very deep.

Out of this bay, he says this king gets his pearls. That he has so great a quantity of pearls that not only are his own skins that he wears decorated with pearls, but also his followers, his beds, and his houses are garnished with them, and great many more besides that it is a wonder to see.

He had some pearls that he said the king gave him when he visited him at Chawanook two years before, he had come because he wanted to trade him pearls for copper. He said they were of the worst kind being black but he was willing to trade because he gave him as many of the black pearls he ask for in trade for his copper. Giving a rope of the oriental looking black pearls, many being very great in size and very round, but they were lost with many other things, coming aboard Drake's fleet.

He also said the king had a great number of pearls that were white, very big, and round. He said the black pearls his men take out of shallow water, but the white pearls his men fish for in very deep water.

It seemed, because of what he said, that the said king had traded with men that had clothes as we have, for these white pearls, and that was the reason that he would only part with black pearls.

King Menatonon promised to give us guides to go over land into that kingdom whenever we wished. He advised to take many men and a lot of food, for he said, that king would not allow any strangers to enter into his kingdom, and never allowing any but his own men to fish for any pearls.

Deciding that if your supplies came before the end of April and if you had sent enough food to last us until the new maize harvest, and if they could stay awhile, we would have enough boats and men to search for the bay of pearls.

A small bark with two pinnaces and two hundred men would go up to the head of the river of Chawanook with the guides that Menatonon would have given, which I was assured would be his best men; as his favorite, beloved son was my prisoner, so I believed him. The prisoner, keeping me company; in a hand lock and his feet were bound together, but loose enough that he could march but not run, for the entire voyage and over land.

The boats would lay waiting for us, protected by twenty-five or thirty guards.

The rest marching with enough food and supplies for two days, hoping to secure enough food every two days for another two-day march. Until we arrived at some convenient place near a maize-field, that we could feed ourselves from. Building a little secure hideout there, guarded by fifteen or twenty men.

From the west, there is a noteworthy river, and in all those parts the most famous, called the River of Moratoc. This river opens into the broad Sound of Weapomeiok. The River of Chawanook, and all the other sounds and bays, salt and fresh, show no current in calm weather, only moved by the wind. This River of Moratoc has such a violent a current from the west and southwest that you can navigate with oars. It has many creeks and turnings, and for the space of over thirty miles rowing, it is as broad as the Thames between Greenwich and the Isle of Dogges.

The Menatonon and even the Moratoc savages report strange things at the head of that river From the town of Moratoc the main town on that river, they say it is thirty or forty days away. They say a spring gushes from a huge rock in such abundance, that it makes a most violent stream, and that this rock is so close to the sea that many times storms cause the fresh water to becomes salty.

After receiving the ransom, we agreed on, his son, Menatonon returned to Roanoke, in the pinnace. I decided to explore that river with about forty men and as much food as I thought we would need until we met with either the Moratoc, or of the Mangoacs which is another tribe of savages, dwelling more to the westward of the said river. We did not get any food from the savages and we were as close to starving as anyone ever was and we had to return before we completed our discovery.

Pemisapan, who changed his name from Wingina upon the death of his brother Granganimeo, had told both the Choanists, and Mangoacs of my purpose coming to them, I having been forced to tell him my reasons so he could serve as guide to the Mangoacs. The whole time he was preparing to come upon us at Roanoke with three thousand men, and that the Mangoacs had also joined them and able to bring as many, if not more.

When we arrived unexpectedly at Chawanook and finding them all together so dismayed them, that it gave us the upper hand.

Pemisapan himself instigated this conference against us and he sent them continual word that our purpose was to destroy them, as Menatonon confessed telling us that they wanted to destroy us.

He also sent them word that the reason why we was passing up their river we were coming to kill them, so that they fled inland taking all of their food and maize.

Since we had already traveled for three days up river, never meeting a man, nor finding any maize in the abandoned town and we only having two days of food left and we were 160 miles from home and suspecting treason, I decided to tell the company about our plight that night before setting the guards on duty. Telling the whole company of the danger, we found ourselves in, betrayed by our own savages lead by Pemmican. The savages, having all fled hoping we would starve to death, lost in the wilderness, being lead so far from home.

That while we still had two days of food, I thought it would be good for us to turn homeward and do what ever was necessary to get to the other side of the of Weapomeiok in time, so we might be able to find something to eat at Chypanum, and the women's town, even though they had been abandoned.

After telling them, asked whether we should continue up the river adventuring, eating all our food, and hoping for a better ending, or should we go back to Roanoke. Asking them to think about it all night, before we decide in the morning which way to go being the direction decided by the most.

The next morning we resolved that while there was even a half pint of maize per person left we would not leave that river, all but three in the opposite opinion. Resolving to eat two days of Sassafras leaves and fast for two days than be drawn back a foot until they saw whether the Mangoacs were friends or enemies.

What made us so desirous of voyaging up the river of Moratoc was to discover where they get a marvelous and most strange mineral. This mine is so notorious amongst them, that all of the savages dwelling up an down the said river, the

Savages of Chawanook, and all them to the westward, but also to all them of the mainland, know of this kingdom's claim to fame, their mine called Chaunis Temoatan.

The mineral they say is Wassador, which is copper, but they call by the name of Wassador every metal.

They say our copper is better then theirs because ours is redder and harder than theirs which is pale and very soft. The metal, carried out of the rocks by a very swift river that falls over rocky hills. They use great bowls and wrap a skin over the hollow part and they take it in shallow water: the manner is this. They take a great bowl and wrap a skin over the hollow end, leaving one part open, that done, they watch the water, and when they see the color change, and they suddenly scoop that water and receives as much ore as the bowl will hold. They cast the ore into a fire, until it melts, yielding five parts, and two parts of metal for three parts of ore.

The Mangoacs have so much of this copper that all of the neighboring Savages report that they beautify their houses with great plates of copper. Believing this to be true, because of not only the reports, but also because of what young Skyko told us.

King of the Chawanooks favorite son Skyko, who was our prisoner also, had been a prisoner of the Mangoacs, being the reason he knew about Chawnis Temoatan. He had never been there because it was 20 days away from the Mangoacs and you had to pass through other kingdoms before coming to the Mangoacs, which would add at least 7 days before reaching Chawnis Temoatan from here.

When questioned the savages that live towards those parts, especially Menatonon, who answered everything asked and promised guides of his own men, who knew the way to Chaunis Temoatan.

He said that the Mangoacs were just a one-day journey by land, from sunup to sundown, from Chawanook; the soonest by water was seven days. The reason to go was to get a sample of the ore for an assay.

However, nothing went as we expected and after two days travel and all of our food gone, we were lying on shore all night and never saw any men, but we could see fires along the shore we were going to pass, until the very last day.

That night about three o'clock we heard savages from shore call Manteo, who was with us in the boat. This made us glad thinking we could have a friendly talk with them, and made Manteo answer them. Soon they began singing, as we thought, in token of our welcome. Manteo after talking to them said they were warning him that they were going to attack us.

We moved to get our light Horsemen ashore, when a volley of arrows started to fly among at us in the boat. Thank God, no one was hurt. Immediately we shot to shore with our hand weapons and landed very easily on a sandy shore ready to secure our place. Which we did even thought the land was a high and steep bluff.

We followed the savages for a short time, until they disappeared into the forest, as the sun was setting.

Having hoped that we could get food from them this was a blow to our company and concerned for our safety, so a strong guard was set and the best sentinels put out.

Deciding to start for Roanoke, the next morning, the whole company in agreement, we left before the rising sun; hoping to be able to make the mouth of the river into the broad sound, not sure if we would escape.

The next night we had rowed until we were four or five miles from the rivers mouth where we stayed on an island, where we had nothing in the world to eat but a soup of

Sassafras leaves, which, as far as commonly know, has never been used as food. The broad sound we had to pass the next day fasting. On Easter Eve, we stayed at the same place, the wind blowing so strong, and the billow of the sail so great, that it would sink the ship if we tried to cross.

Easter morning we continued to fast but the wind became calm and by four o'clock, we came to Chipanum. All of the savages had fled but we were able to get some fish from their traps thank God. The next morning we arrived at Roanoke.

Reporting the details of this voyage was so that you will know that every man tried his best, suffering greatly, to try to find the pearl oyster bed and the copper- mine for you.

Even with out the discovery of either of the two it will still be the sweetest and healthful climate, and soil offering many things like Sassafras, and many other roots and other good things that will make good merchandise. Provided we find a better harbor, hoping to do so this summer for this river of Moratoc promises great things.

Thus Sir, though simply, yet truly set down for you, what our labors, not without both pain and peril, has yielded for you, but not as much as could have been done, if what you had provided for us had been left with us. Or that the great most strange & unlooked for storm had not carried away all of our provisions and personal belongings and everything, so courteously supplied by General Sir Francis Drake, which would have been sufficient to perform the greatest part of our mission. The storm also taking away our barks with its Master and its sailors and some of our own company, making us think that God must have saved the rest of us on purpose for some reason.

The Second Part: Touching The Conspiracy Of Wingina, Who Changed His Name To Pemisapan, The Discovery Of The Same, And At The Last, Of Our Request To Depart With General Sir Francis Drake For England

Ensinore, a Savage, father to Pemisapan being our only friend with the King's ear died the 20 of April 1586. He alone had opposed both the King and all the rest of them, when they wanted revenge against us, in retaliation for the destruction of Aquascogoc.

King Piemacum decided to follow the advice of his ministers, to leave the area, so we could not force them to feed us and we would starve to death.

March 1586 Piemacum, with all his savages ran away from us, without planting the maize gardens. Except for a miracle from the hand of God, we would starve. For at that time we had not one grain of maize to plant in the ground and we had no traps for fish, lacking the skill to make them.

In my absence, on my voyage that I had made against the Choanists and Mangoacs, both had been telling lies among the other savages that they had fought us, and part of our men slain, and part of our men starved to death. Until our return, Pemisapan and his followers believed them holding us now in contempt and no longer under a delusion that we are Gods.

When I returned, Pemisapan was surprised that the rumors were not true, which he could not doubt, because not only were we alive, but also by report of three of his own Savages which had been with me on that voyage besides Manteo, Tetepano, Cossine, and his sister's husband Eracano.

The Choanists and Mangoacs have a reputation that they have the most fighting men who are terrifying being the strongest and the bravest, so none of the other savages dare fight them.

Nevertheless, we did fight them and most ran away, but the ones that stayed and fought, we killed and we took their king Menatonon prisoner, and brought his son that he loves best to Roanoke, as our prisoner.

Discovering all this some of Pemisapan's men had more respect for our powers because they could not deny what they could see.

It made the wisest amongst them, and their old men, to remember Elsinore's opinions with greater respect.

For he often told them we were the servants of God, and could not be destroyed by them; that just the opposite would happen and anyone who tried to kill us were asking for their own death.

Some days after our return Menatonon sent a messenger to visit his prisoner son and sent pearls for a present, as Pemisapan believed, for the ransom of his son, therefore, leaving us no choice but to refuse them.

He did not know the real reason he sent them, being an agreed sign, that he had commanded King Okisco, of Weopomeiok, to yield himself servant, and pay homage to the great Wiroanza of England, and after her to Sir Walter Raleigh.

He also sent twenty-four of his principal men to Pemisapan, at Roanoke as a sign, they were ready to perform the ceremony to acknowledge that from that time forward, he, and his successors acknowledged her Majesty as their only sovereign, and next to her, Raleigh.

After that, Pemisapan seemed to change his mind in opposition toward us causing his men to set up fish traps for us and by the end of April, he had sowed a large maize garden, enough to feed our whole company for a whole year. Besides that, he gave us a plot of land for our own. All of this would put us in marvelous comfort, if we could pass from April until the beginning of July, which was to have been the beginning of their harvest.

All our fear was over the two months between, if the savages should stop helping us with meat and eatables and our traps should fail us, as often they did, we might starve. As the proverb goes, about the starving horse locked in the stable watching the growing green grass just outside the barn door. Notwithstanding the growing maize, we knew we could hardly escape starvation; except by the hand of God, as it pleased him to help us.

A few days after all of that Ensinore our friend died and no sooner, dead, but certain of our great enemies especially; Oscan, Tanaquiny, and Wanchese, were again turning them against us, which most were ready to do: Renewing all of their former mischief against us with mainly new suggestions of ways to starve us.

The Weopomeiok, in their savage manner, hold a special funeral ceremony when a great person dies. It is set at a certain date so that all of the neighboring kingdoms are able to attend, to pay their respects to the deceased.

The tenth of June was the date set for Elsinore's funeral. At this instant, the Mandoages, the Chesepians, and their friends were on their way with 700 fighting men, armed and arriving altogether on the mainland at the town Dasamonquepeuc, across from Roanoke Island, the main part of a plan to destroy us on the appointed date.

Their plan called for lighting signal fires along the shore once they were in place. Once seeing the fires of theirs, Pemisapan would light fires on the opposite side along the shore of Roanoke as a signal that they had killed me, and some of our "Wiroances," their name for all our principal officers.

Seeing the signaling fires the main forces would then come

to the island, to kill the rest of the company, who were scattered around the Island to live, seeking crabs and fish trying not to starve to death.

Tarraquine and Andacon, two principal advisor's of Pemisapan, and very healthy, vigorous fellows, with twenty fighting men, were appointed to kill me by setting fire to the reed roof on my house, in the middle of the night and when I ran out in my shirt without weapons, they would use their clubs to knock out my brains.

The same order then given to all of others to do the same to Master Herriot, all of the other houses, and the fort: To set everything on fire and at the same instant kill everyone falling into the trap. This being the only way to deal with us, as just ten of us, well armed, could kill hundreds of them.

First, King Okisco, of Weopomeiok, and Mandoages move in an orderly manner and with a great quantity of copper to the number of seven, or eight hundred bowls filled with copper.

However, the savages would not trade us any food for any amount of copper whatsoever: even though copper was to them more precious than gold or silver is to us.

Besides that in the night, they robbed the traps they had built us and then broke them, and once broken they would never repair them again.

This way, Pemisapan was sure we scattered our men and he was not disappointed because famine was wearing us down to the extreme.

I sent Captain Stafford with 20 men to Croatan, my Lord Admiral's island, to serve two purposes in one. That is to say, to feed himself and his company, and also to keep watch and let us know if he saw any ships coming up the coast.

Master Pridiox took the pinnace to Hatterask, and ten men and the Provost Marshal with him to live there, also to wait for shipping. In addition, every week 16 or 20 of the rest of the company went to the mainland, to hunt and live off oysters.

In the meantime, Pemisapan left Roanoke for two reasons: One to plant his second crop: the other to prevent my daily sending to him for a supply of food for my company, for he was afraid to deny me any thing, or dare make excuses.

Content to accept his refusing to feed us, this time, because we had reason to have him there to ambush him; in the meanwhile doing what we had never done before we put up with it.

Our purpose was to ally with Menatonon, and the Choanists, who in truth are people that are more valiant, and in greater number than the rest. They are more faithful in their promises, and they had an earnest desire to join in league with us. They were therefore greatly offended with Pemisapan and Weopomeiok for making them believe such tales of us.

The third cause of this going to Dasamonquepeuc was to dispatch his messengers to Weopomeiok, and to the Mandoages about the plan to destroy us: all which he did with impressive amounts of copper in hand, making large promises to them of greater spoils.

Once the date for the funeral ceremony at Roanoke was set, the invitation sent to every kingdom, their answers came in a few days.

The Weopomeiok divided into two parties; first King Okisco refused to be of Pemisapan's party for himself, or any of his especial followers. Therefore, they did not go to the mainland for the funeral, they knowing it being only a pretext for an attack to destroy us. The rest of the Weopomeiok accepted: and so did the Mandoages, as Wanchese had turned them into our enemies, along with Pemisapan.

Skyko, the son of King Menatonon and our prisoner, told

all of this after he tried to run away catching him and laid him over a log, threatening to cut off his head.

Reminding the young fellow how well we all treated him; he told what he had learned, which was confirmed by one of Pemisapan's own men, captured the night before Pemisapan was slain.

Finding out this plot to destroy all of us and with our company scattered so far; we had to prevent them from executing their plan.

Sending to Pemisapan, to put suspicion out of his head that our fleet had arrived and we were going to go to Croatan. However, in truth we had not heard nor hoped for such good news. Telling him we were coming to borrow some of his men to fish and hunt for us at Croatan and to buy four days of food for the voyage.

He sent word he would come over to Roanoke himself, but day after day, he failed to come, waiting for the Weopomeiok and the Mandoages, who was expect within eight days.

It was the last of May 1586 when all his own savages began to make their assembly at Roanoke, at his command, to join him in his plan.

Deciding not to wait, but to go the next day and visit him with such men as we had. That night we canvassed the island and seized all of the canoes to keep anyone from informing Pemisapan of our intentions.

The town received warning anyway because of the Master of the light Horsemen. Sent with a few men to gather up all the canoes at sunset, then to go to Dasamonquepeuc with instructions to take anyone trying to leave and prevent any one trying to land.

On the crossing over, he met with a canoe coming from the island shore, turned over the canoe and cut off the heads of two Savages who were in the canoe.

This happened not far from the shore and a cry of alarm arose from the shore because they had sentinels spying on us as we had sentinels spying on them.

Just as the alarm sounded, they armed themselves with their bows and arrows, and we our weapons. Immediately we killed three or four, the rest fled into the woods.

The next morning, we went to Dasamonquepeuc, with the light Horsemen from the night before, and with another canoe taking 25 men with our Sergeant Major, and the Colonel of the Chesepians.

Landing, one of Pemisapan's own Savages took a message to Pemisapan to come to a meeting at the shore. Being on the way to Croatan, and meant to take him with us to complain to him about Oscan, caught the past night, carrying away our prisoner, whom was there, tied in a hand-lock.

The king wanted me to come to him, and finding my self amidst seven or eight of his principal Wiroances and followers, I gave the watch-word agreed upon, which was, "Christ our victory!" and immediately his chief men and himself received what they had planned for us.

The king himself, shot by the Colonel with a pistol, was lying on the ground for dead. I was looking for Manteo's friends to save them and our men were busy that none of the rest escaped.

Suddenly King Pemisapan jumped up, and ran away as though he had not been touched, out running all of the company, even after shot in the buttocks, to disappear into the woods.

In the end an Irish man, one Edward Nugent, and the deputy provost, followed him into the woods. For a while, thinking we had lost both the king and my man, by our own negligence, having been discovered by the Savages; when, we met Nugent returning out of the woods carrying by the hair Pemisapan's head in his hand.

This happened June 1, 1586, June 8 Captain Stafford, living at my lord Admiral's Island, sent word he had discovered a great fleet of twenty three sails: but whether they were friends or Spanish foes, he could not yet tell, advising to post as good of a guard as possible.

June 9 he himself came, having travelled day and night to travel the twenty miles. Truly, any report of him from the first to the last would say; he is a Gentleman, works hard, and faces peril by land or water, fair weather or foul, to perform any service given him.

He brought a letter from the General Sir Francis Drake, with a most bountiful and honorable offer to supply us with everything we needed to perform our mission.

He not only gave us food, ammunition and clothing, but also barks, pinnaces, and boats; furnished with supplies, food, and men.

June 10 he arrived at our bad harbor, coming there to anchor. June 11 we met and I found him indeed most honorably and willing to perform that which he offered in writing and by message, he having already consulted with all of the captains of his fleet and gotten their consent, they liking the proposal to stay with us.

We tried to thank General Drake as best we could, but was not able to thank him as well as he deserved.

Also craved at his hands, that if he would please take with him back to England some who were ill suited to be here, and others weak and unfit for my good mission, and in their place, supply me with replacements; ship Masters, Cavilers, and others more suitable for our rigorous and dangerous mission.

Having received the request, he provided two pinnaces and

four small boats supplied with everything we needed, and all of our food, to last us until about next August, a year from now. Not only would that help us perform our mission, but will help carry us back to England when the time should come, but also enable me to search the coast for a better harbor.

When all of the provisions and the men and everything else were aboard our barks, having accepted their charge from the General a terrible tempest arrived, staying for four days, from June13 through June 16.

If God had not raised his hand over them and the General not put them out to sea, the whole fleet would have been tossed and destroyed on the dangerous shore.

The Francis, with all provisions, two Masters, and some of our company aboard was lost; broke freed from her anchor, and driven out into the sea.

The General came ashore making a new offer to provide, again, food sufficient to carry us through and a ship of 170 ton, called the Bark Bonner, with a Master and guide. Adding he would not for any thing, bring her into our harbor and therefore he would leave the rest up to us.

He advised to take counsel with the rest of the company, and then deliver in writing what ever we required, and he would do all in his power to satisfy us, adding his assurances to us that his Captains, and he, would most willingly satisfy our requests.

The Captains and Gentlemen of our company, who were all there when the General made his offer to us, gave their opinions. Their request was that considering our case, the weakness and small number of our company, the carrying away of our bark, with two special Masters, our principal provisions, and our personal belongings, by the very hand of God it seemed. Now, considering his second offer, though honorable on his part, still we should not take it, as it was not possible to bring her to our harbor.

Furthermore, our hoped for supplies being past due, Sir Richard Grenville, promising us his return before Easter, and now two months late and not likely to come this year.

Accordingly, written requests for the General in all our names to, please, provide passage to England with him. He most readily agreed, and immediately his pinnaces arrived at our island to fetch away the few left there with our baggage.

The weather was so boisterous, and the pinnaces so often scrapping ground, the sailors cast overboard most of all we had, with all our cards, books, and writings.

The General, in the name of the Almighty, sailed for England with relief, because he was in more peril relieving us than in all of his former actions against the Spanish.

We set sail June 19, 1586, and arrived in Portsmouth, England July 27, 1586.

Signed, Ralph Lane

"Nana, did that really happen?" questioned Adam, a little doubt in his voice.

"I don't believe they would dare lie to the Queen or to Raleigh, do you?"

"Not if they wanted to keep their heads," Adam replied with conviction.

Raleigh Syndicates America's First Real Estate Development

"Raleigh's real estate development was the first Adam, but it wasn't much different from most real estate developments today, being more often than not that the original developers pay the cost while the new owners down the line reaps the benefits.

"At this time, Raleigh was wealthy from pirating and from his estates in Ireland where he is credited for planting the first potatoes. It's a good thing Raleigh is rich, considering how expensive it was to be Raleigh. Living the courtly life in the Elizabethan age meant expensive clothes, homes, servants, and lavish and entertaining parties, and for Raleigh, also paying for expensive exploration missions and planting colonies.

"After the disastrous first attempt at settling a colony Raleigh decided to set up a syndicate to sell shares in his second attempt to establish a colony.

"Because Lane and the others left the colony with Drake, Raleigh believed that if the members of the colony had a stake in the syndicate they would work harder for success. This time he setup a syndicate named The Virginia Company, this time the Governor is John White.

"The syndicate was a real estate business enterprise to establish a colony in Virginia, its shares sold to investors, consisting of a Governor, and 12 Assistants, who will oversee the colonization of the City of Raleigh in Virginia.

"In addition, the syndicate promises each man who would settle the colony at least 500 acres each; selecting 150 people: 124 men, 17 wives, and 9 children, who are now called planters, and as required in Raleigh's Charter a fifth share of all gold and silver found is reserved for the Crown."

Nana sighed, "Adam, it's too bad they didn't follow Raleigh's written directions to settle in the Chesapeake Bay area where there were better ports and different Indians.

"This time it only takes 17 days before they make a blunder. By the way Adam, blunder means: A huge, stupid, careless mistake.

"May 8, 1587 the fleet of three ships sailed for Virginia.

"July 22, 1587 Governor John White was on the first ship

to arrive on Croatan Island. It was renamed Hatteras Island much later.

"While waiting for the others Governor White and a small group of planters visited Roanoke Island, looking for the 15 men left there by Grenville.

"They only found the bones of one of them who had been killed by the Indians.

"The next day, they went to the north end of the island, where Lane had built the fort and the houses the year before.

"The Indians had torn down the fort but did not hurt the houses. Melons were growing inside and deer were inside eating the melons, appearing as though no one had lived there for a very long time and no sign of Grenville's men on the island.

"The Indians who had lived on Roanoke Island and the other followers of Pemisapan, and the other tribes all stayed away and White had to ask Manteo for help.

"Adam, it's thought that Manteo's mother was queen of the Croatans, so when Manteo tried to influence his friends and his relatives on Croatan Island they became friendlier, but not the other Indian tribes.

"The Croatans told White that a few Indians had not been killed by Lane at Dasamonquepeuc, and after Grenville left they killed all 15 of the men Grenville had left behind.

"August 8, 1587 Governor White, Captain Stafford, and 24 men launch a surprise attack on Dasamonquepeuc, killing almost everyone and setting it on fire.

"Adam, this blunder causes a crisis for the colony and Manteo. The other Indians had all ran away after White's fleet arrived.

"Learning the others had run away the Croatan Indians went there looking for any food left behind. White and his men had killed Manteo's friends and relatives who were there taking the melons.

"Manteo was their loyal friend; probably the last true Indian friend the planters had. He tried to convince his relatives it was a mistake and the Croatan Indians said they forgave the mistake, but they probably were pretending for Manteo's sake.

"On August 13, Manteo was baptized and in a ceremony made Lord of Roanoke and Dasamonquepeuc as a reward from Raleigh for his many services.

"August 18, Governor White's granddaughter Virginia Dare was born.

"The few Croatan Indians left willing to help them because of Manteo could not help enough so a month and two days after arriving Governor White left on August 27, 1587, sailing with the fleet when it returned to England to bring back needed supplies and more planters.

"The year 1588 was the year of the Spanish Armada War, and war could not have come at a worst time for the colony. Raleigh, Drake, and Grenville and all their ships were in the fight to save England.

"Raleigh signed the deed March 7, 1589; selling his share in the Virginia Company to John White and his associates who still wanted to settle the colony.

"I didn't find out how much Raleigh sold his Virginia Company for Adam but I'm sure he must have been happy with the deal just to get rid of it."

"I think he was glad to get rid of it, too, Nana, because it was expensive. I don't want to spend all of my money for real estate even when it's just Monopoly® money," confided Adam.

"There is something we know they didn't know Adam; No one knows it will take White 2 years and 355 days before he returns alone and empty-handed and discovers everyone missing.

"You can read all about it in your boring details section, Nana," teased Adam.

The Colony Is Lost, And Raleigh Goes To Prison For Love

"Adam, England's war with Spain required every ship, and even with Raleigh's help White was unable to get the transportation to deliver the desperately needed supplies and more planters they needed to increase the strength of the colony against the Indians.

"Another year passes, and still White is desperately seeking transportation when he comes up with a scheme and begs Raleigh to intercede for them at court. The plan being that if Raleigh could help Master John Watte get clearances for his fleet of privateers wanting to sail to the West Indies to plunder the Spanish, they would take White, the planters, and supplies to Virginia.

"All of those plans fell through, some blamed Raleigh's enemies at court because they wanted his colony to fail, but finally White was allowed to sail on one of Watte's ships, leaving England on March 20, 1590 but only as a passenger, not being allowed to carry supplies or more planters with him.

"Captain Watte wanted to go pirating in the West Indies first, finally on the night of August 12, 1590 Watte's fleet anchors at the northeast end of Roanoke Island.

"They see smoke coming from several areas along the shores and on August 16, White, Captain Cooke, Captain Spicer, and a few men in two boats go to investigate but with great effort find the smoke is from smoldering forest fires, and they can see smoke rising from Roanoke Island.

"The next day they prepare to go to Roanoke but Spicer and six men drown when their boat capsizes.

"After much persuasion, White is allowed to continue the search, and they put off again in two boats. It's dark when they get to Roanoke and they land a quarter of a mile from where White left the colony.

"They see a light and setting anchor opposite it and in the dark they blow a trumpet and sing songs but see no signs of life. With daylight they land on the north end of the island and find out the light and smoke were from grass fires and several rotten trees burning.

"White searched the shore where they had kept their small boats but found them all gone but he did see footprints of two or three Indians left there the night before.

"They went through the woods, passing through the area that was directly opposite Dasamonquepeuc on the mainland, where they had killed Pemisapan and all around the island until they came to the colony.

"Adam, it must have been eerie, finding the colony deserted and his daughter and grand daughter missing, but with the word Croatan carved into a main post and CRO carved into a tree trunk on the path outside the settlement, White hoped his family and the others were with Manteo on Croatan Island.

"They could see that all of the houses and been torn down and heavy cast-iron objects scattered around and overgrown with grass and weeds they could tell that no one had lived there for a long time.

"White found his trunk that he had secretly buried before he left. The Indians had dug it up his papers, books, and drawings and all were ruined by the weather.

"Then they were forced by bad weather to return to their ships. It was still stormy the next day so Captain Watte decided they would go to the West Indies for fresh food and water and then come back to Croatan Island, but they were blown off course and had to return to England.

"Then, in July 1592, trouble starts for Raleigh when Queen Elizabeth 1 finds out he had married Elizabeth Throckmorton who was one of her Ladies-in-Waiting without her permission.

"The Queen orders both Raleigh and his wife imprisoned in the Tower of London but she releases them when one of Raleigh's ships brings back a huge treasure trove, plundered from the captured Spanish ship Madre de Dios.

"White was unable to come up with anymore financing and died February 4, 1593, without finding out what had happened to the lost colony.

"Then Raleigh talks the Queen into letting him search for the city of El Dorado and on February 6, 1595 Raleigh leaves England on his first expedition searching for the famous 'Lost City of Gold'.

"Unfortunately, the expedition was a total failure and Raleigh and his wife lived secluded lives at his estate until the queen died. That's when real trouble starts for Raleigh, Adam; this time Raleigh loses Virginia and his head."

Raleigh Goes Back To Prison, This Time For Treason

"After the queen's death on March 24, 1603 Raleigh was again imprisoned in the tower. This time it was for plotting against her replacement King James I," explained Nana.

"In 1607 King James set up his first syndicate even though there were concerns that some of Raleigh's planters might be alive, which meant that Raleigh would have fulfilled his obligation to plant a colony and Raleigh would still own Virginia.

"This time the syndicate was for the founding of Jamestown in the Chesapeake area, of course named after the king.

"The planters blundered there as badly as the others and if kindhearted Pocahontas had not saved Captain John Smith they all would have starved to death during what was called the 'starving years' and it would have become a lost colony, too.

"In 1612 Raleigh promises King James 1 a fortune if he allows him to leave prison to go on another expedition to search for the 'Lost City of Gold'.

"In 1616 the king finally frees Raleigh to lead the second expedition but it also fails and as they were returning to England Raleigh's men plundered a Spanish outpost.

"Adam, the expedition could not have ended any worse because when the Spanish complained against Raleigh King James 1 was eager to keep the peace and saw it as an opportunity to take back Virginia and ordered Raleigh arrested for treason.

"Being convicted of treason is an important point because of those concerns that some of Raleigh's planters might still be alive his relatives would have inherited Virginia.

"Adam being convicted for treason meant that Raleigh lost everything, Virginia, Ireland and his English estates and on October 29, 1618 he even lost his head."

"Nana, no offense, but are you certain they cut off Sir Walter Raleigh's head?"

"Adam, you can read all about Raleigh on England's royal website where it tells about how Raleigh's body was buried but his head was embalmed, placed in a leather bag, and then sent to his widow."

Shocked Adam remarked, "Nana, it's hard to believe that a king would put anyone's head into a leather bag and send it to his wife because it doesn't make any sense to do that to his wife."

"It does seem senseless to be so cruel," agreed Nana. Trying to change the subject, Nana suggested, "Let's look at Raleigh's old map. When you compare it with our 2007 map of North Carolina, you can see that Croatan Island is now Hatteras Island. Look, Rodanthe is on Hatteras Island Adam. That's where the Nicholas Sparks book *Nights in Rodanthe* takes place.

"And right down from there is Ocracoke Island where Blackbeard gets beheaded."

Imagine You A Swindler

Carolina, The Land Of Opportunity For Rascals And Swindlers

"Swindle means to cheat victims out of money by using a believable lie to trick them.

"In other words, Adam a swindle is the business plan of a rascal who is dishonest, who perfectly knows the laws, but instead of applying brakes on their brains to keep from cheating cheats anyway to get money.

"As long as they get away with it they believe they are being clever and obviously they have no conscience. They don't care they are causing real trouble and hurting innocent people with their schemes, otherwise, out of compassion and ethics they would stop.

"Adam, when our Baron bought the land from the Lords Proprietors to found New Bern there was no real estate ownership like we have now.

"Back then the Crown had to grant a patent for land before anyone had any right or a claim to it. And a grant was not a sale of the land like real estate ownership is today it was only a kind of land-lease agreement with a tenant who would be required to pay rent, but their right to use the land could be inherited.

"These grants all held high expectations of making money from rents and the tenants would also owe money having to do with things they bought and sold because of taxes, duties, customs, stamps, fees, and fines, and other ways the colony and settlers might owe money to the Crown and to the Lord Proprietors, year after year.

"The sooner they made money for the mother country the better. To make money they needed to plant colonies with people developing the land, so there was pressure was on the Lords Proprietors to grant land to as many tenants as possible.

"Each grant included a yearly quit-rent due to the Crown. A quit-rent meant that the tenants paid money instead of having to provide services to the Crown that otherwise they would have been required to perform. Even if no one paid rent to the Lords Proprietors, the Lords Proprietors would still owe the Crown its share of the rents.

"We can see how important it was for the Lords Proprietors to put in charge people who would be loyal to them, and honest and trustworthy enough to not become tempted by greed and cheat them.

"The feudal system and Carolina's Fundamental Constitution were quite complicated and I'm just trying to make this part simple so you can understand the swindle. After King George III granted Carolina to the Lords Proprietors, they subdivided Carolina into smaller parcels of land that they would then grant to others, like their grants to our Baron' and his Swiss Colony.

"Adam, what seemed so wonderful about our Baron's New Bern colony was that he was bringing his tenants with him, silver mines were waiting, and friendly Indians were eager to trade their furs, and Europe was just as eager to buy them. To make it perfect the John Ritter Company, his partners in Bern, Switzerland, had his back so failure seemed impossible.

"Success seemed so certain that even today some still misjudge and blame our Baron for what happened during New Bern's first two years. Some have even publicly insulted our Baron for trying to defend himself with his explanations about what he thinks happened.

"Our Baron was only trying to tell us his side of the story and it's important to remember that our Baron had been conned and he never learned the whole truth, even though he mentions a 'rascally gang' in his manuscript.

Adam con means to swindle or trick so it is no wonder that our Baron was very surprised when he got here and found himself in the middle of a very disagreeable situation and things got worse and more dangerous as time past.

"Now we can see that our Baron didn't know the whole truth. That the silver mines were a lie, that there had been a total collapse of the government and anarchy and other disturbing things had been going on for years. Like stealing the Indian's land and kidnapping Indians in order to sell them into slavery, causing the Indians to want revenge and to go on the warpath.

"Adam, anarchy means a society without a government. That is important because without the control of a government there are no courts or justice and political confusion results when some people take matters into their own hands in order to try to get power for themselves.

"The main problem with criticizing our Baron's writing about his side of the story is that you can tell that our Baron didn't have a clue about the 'back-story'. Adam, maybe we can help clear our Baron's name in our book."

"How can we do that Nana," quizzed Adam.

"The same way we learned the true story about what happened around here, from the colonial records. We could include the different clues we found and once a reader has enough clues, revealing the rascals actions, then maybe they will also be able to see the truth.

"Think of history as a giant picture puzzle, you need all of the pieces put together to see the big picture and if key pieces are missing you are just guessing at the truth.

"Believe me I know. I held opinions based on what some popular historians and writers assumed until I read the facts.

"When I learned what some of the key players were actually doing, those facts changed what I thought about everything, especially about Lawson."

"And actions speak louder than words Nana," observed Adam with a smile, "and if we follow their actions we will be following in their footsteps."

"Great points Adam, let's get started, but the story gets complicated so I hope you will not think it's boring. However," Nana admitted with a sigh, "I am afraid it is going to wind up in the boring section."

Moving his chair closer to the computer, he replied, "Okay, Nana, I will try to think it is interesting, but I am not going to promise anything."

Nana began speaking in a soft voice tone, as if she were sad to admit what had happened, "In reality, it was impossible for our Baron to succeed and he never learned the whole truth about his adventure to America. He only knew that his last adventure ended in disaster and it made him sad for the rest of his life.

"Even though about half of his colony never made it here, the Indians were alarmed seeing so many strangers moving in on them all at once. Especially, since they were fighting-age men with guns who wanted the Neusiok to move from their home village of Chatooka so they could live there instead."

"Nana if a lot of strange people came to New Bern and told us to move I wouldn't like it either."

"Adam I'm glad to hear you say that, empathy is important if you want to understand these true stories about some of Carolina's land swindles and the calamities they caused.

"The land swindle Lawson was involved in is important because of the huge tracts of land belonging to many different Indian tribes and the hundreds of people they duped into buying it, and because the grant process involves many people. "But Lawson wasn't the mastermind."

Choose Your Politicians Wisely; They Can Get You Killed!

"Adam, in the beginning there was no North Carolina or South Carolina. Carolina was so large that Carolina's governor sent a deputy governor to the northern part, known as the Albemarle area, since many settlers were already living there.

"Edward Moseley, Esquire, in particular, lived there, he received thousands of acres in grants for his plantations, but he also illegally took up huge tracts of Indians lands had the tracts surveyed apart into smaller parcels then sold them to unsuspecting dupes."

"Its important to point out that there's no doubt Moseley knew very well that he didn't have any rights to the land he was selling. He was an important and very wealthy attorney, who owned thousands of acres of land and was North Carolina's Surveyor General, on and off, for many years.

"He also held many very important government positions

for Carolina and for his Precinct over many years. His most important positions were being a Deputy Lord Proprietor and Speaker of Carolina's General Assembly.

"During the time Lawson knew him, Moseley was one of the most powerful and influential attorneys and government officials in Carolina. He was such a talented speaker they repeatedly made him Speaker of the General Assembly.

"The Speaker is in charge and sets the agenda for the Assembly so you can see why he was one of Carolina's most powerful citizens and why people would try to please him in order to have their concerns and desires brought before the Assembly.

"Not only that, Moseley knew the procedures: First the Governor or Governor's Council issued a Warrant for the proportions and location of the land granted, then gave the Warrant to the surveyor to survey the land.

"The surveyor, after marking out the boundaries of the land on the ground, gives a Certificate to the Secretary certifying the quantity of land and a small plot map showing its proportions and location.

"Then the Secretary records the Certificate in a bound book kept for that reason only and certifies to the Governor or to the Governor and the Certificate Council what the surveyor did.

"Next, the Governor orders the Secretary to draw-up a Guarantee, Seal it with North Carolina's Seal, and send it and the plot map to the buyer so he will know his land has been laid out and recorded for him and his heirs.

"The swindle is one thing, but that's not to say that they never made any legitimate grants of land belonging to the Lords Proprietors. However, the rascals had no right to sell land that belonged to the Indians and that caused all of the trouble.

"The swindle began years before our Baron moved here. They were selling land belonging to the Maherine Indians, who lived along the dividing-line between Virginia and Carolina and by treaty were subjects of England, as well as other tribal lands.

"Although most of the buyers ran the Indians off with violence some people wanted to do the right thing and paid the Indians to go away, like our Baron did when he paid the Neusiok to move away from Chatooka.

"I believe that it is fair to say that Moseley was a 'secret double-agent' Adam, because he was on Cary's side trying to overthrow the Lords Proprietors even though he was a sworn Deputy Lord Proprietor charged to protect the Lords Proprietors' interest.

"Not only that, Carolina's Fundamental Constitution says, 'No person whatever, shall hold or claim any land in Carolina, by purchase or gift, or otherwise, from the natives or any other whatsoever; but merely from and under the Lords Proprietors, upon pain of forfeiture of all his estate, moveable or immoveable, and perpetual banishment'.

"So it's clear that Moseley was merely posing as a Deputy Lord Proprietor while he was defrauding them and the Indians and, because of the necessary surveys, Lawson was right in the middle of it.

"That brazen real estate swindle that so many died over is well documented and Moseley lived for another 38 years after Lawson died; but important records had been stolen by Cary and it took over a hundred years before Carolina could finally gather together copies of Carolina's missing colonial records that told the whole story.

"These stories are true Adam because they're the facts. They are also good examples of why you should start at the beginning and research the official records yourself if you really want to know the truth.

"Adam, if you just researched the history of your hometown starting when John Lawson moved here, and you read his book and read what our Baron wrote about his American adventure here, you still would not know the whole story about how the Golden Rule saved our Baron's life and how revenge killed Lawson.

Indians Never Forgot A Kindness And Never Forgave A Wrong

"Adam if you just limited your research to what some authors said about it in their books or in articles where they wrote about Lawson and his book you might accept their conclusions that he was an advocate for the Indians and maybe he was in his book. His book was to lure more people to Carolina. More people meant more buyers for their real estate development swindle, more surveys, and more money for Lawson and his friends.

"Lawson was smart, and right after Lawson arrived in the Albemarle area, in February 1701, Moseley became his mentor and soon Lawson was working for Moseley as a surveyor.

"Lawson knew what was going on, but more important, Lawson is the one the Indians see surveying their stolen land apart.

"These are just some of the important jobs and government positions Lawson held during the 11 years he lived here.

"By 1703-1704, Deputy Governor, Landgrave Robert Daniell, Esquire had appointed Lawson as the Surveyor for Bath County. In addition, when Moseley became Surveyor General he made Lawson his Deputy Surveyor for North

Carolina. By 1709, the Lords Proprietors had appointed Lawson Surveyor General for North Carolina.

"Lawson was a very busy surveyor but he was also Precinct Commissioner, Registrar, and Clerk of Court of Bath County from 1706 until 1708, when Carolina's legitimate government collapsed and closed the courts. Just let me point out here that Lawson's government positions were important to the swindlers, you might even say the rascals were in control of the situation, inside and out.

"There's plenty of colonial documents complaining for years, especially the Maherine Indians, to: their Majesties, Virginia's Governor Spotswood, The Board of Trade of England, Carolina's Lords Proprietors, Carolina's Governors, and others about the violence against the Indians, as a result of the hundreds of illegal surveys involved in taking away the Maherine, Pamlico, Neusiok, Coree and other Tuscarora Indian's lands.

"Adam, the Indians were being forced away with violence from their homes and hunting grounds because they were occupying Carolina's most beautiful and fruitful locations beside the rivers and creeks.

"Now the thing about all of that is this, Lawson gave those settlers the same advice he gave to our Baron, being to not pay the Indians for their land but to 'run them off' instead, because that's what the settlers did.

"Creating hostilities on both sides and the Indians' desire for revenge grew as the rascals sold more land and hundreds of settlers moved in.

"Not only that, and even though orders from the Crown and the Lords Proprietors, to treat the Indians well and to develop a good relationship with them for trading their animal furs, matters were made worse when as many Indians as possible were set upon, assaulted and captured so they could be enslaved. Which I might add did not take much to encourage the practice since it was a source of income for poor settlers.

"However, some writers just casually mention 'stealing Indian lands and enslaving them' and by glossing over these facts, as if they were no big deal, proves they did not research deep enough, or worse could not correctly interpret important facts that lead to anarchy and war. Instead, they settle on blaming our Baron for everything because of what they thought he should have done.

"Our Baron wrote that after they were captured and held prisoner, the chiefs who lived along the Pamlico, Neuse, and Chowan Rivers and the Coree tribe were the main ones who accused Lawson of stealing their land. At that Indian tribal council, and after hearing all the evidence, the chiefs all agreed that Lawson deserved their worst punishment.

"Adam, Indians thought it was no punishment to die and go to Skyland so when they wanted to punish those they had condemned to death they would choose a horrific way to die.

"I read a letter that Christopher Gale wrote November 2, 1711, saying that he would have been with our Baron and Lawson on the trip but he had to go home because his wife and brother became deathly ill. He wrote that he learned how they killed Lawson. Gale described how the Indians 'stuck him full of torchwood, like hog bristles', and thinks he would have suffered the same fate as Lawson if he had not gone home. I think he felt that way because he worried that the Indians knew about his involvement in stealing their land.

"Others described how the Indians pinched together a piece of his skin and thrust a pitch-pine splinter through it until his whole body looked like a grotesque porcupine. Then they tied him to a post around which a circle of fire was set near his feet. Then they danced around him, kicking the red-hot coals towards his bare feet until the splinters around his ankles caught fire and then watched him 'dance', as the flames spread to nearby splinters, the fires slowly climbing up his body until he died in an unimaginable agony.

"Some blame our Baron for saving himself and not saving Lawson but the truth is our Baron could not have saved Lawson; even Lawson knew that an Indian never forgot a kindness and never forgave a wrong.

Old Enough To Know Right From Wrong

"It's thought that Lawson was born in December of 1674, but it doesn't matter, we'll just say that in 1700 Lawson was a young man in his mid-twenties. You know old enough to know right from wrong.

"It doesn't matter where Lawson went to school or if he attended free outdoor lectures at Gresham College in London, as some like to argue about. None of that's important because it's apparent from his accomplishments and rapid advancements in Carolina's government that Lawson's education was good enough for a clever young man.

"In 1700, while Lawson was in London, there's no doubt that he was trying to meet people who could help him launch his career. Networking is what enterprising young people still do today. You have to be careful though Adam because others know you by the company you seek and the friends you keep.

"Being an adventurer and wanting to travel he followed the advice he received from his networking efforts in London that Carolina was just the place for him, and he kept a journal during his travels through wild Carolina that he turn into his now famous book, *A New Voyage to Carolina*.

"Lawson knew Carolina's seat of government for northern Carolina was in the Albemarle area, which was known as the' mother settlement' because it was the first, and he planned his journey to end there.

"Lawson hooks up with Moseley and meets other influential people and important northern Carolina officials, because most of them live around the Albemarle area.

"Including two of Carolina's Deputy Governors, Landgrave Daniel, Esquire and Thomas Cary, Esquire; Chief Justice and Receiver General for all of the Lords Proprietors money in Carolina, Christopher Gale, Esquire, who will become Lawson's attorney when Landgrave Daniel sues Lawson for swindling him. Some even suggest they met in England and that Gale was the one who encouraged him to move to Carolina.

"But all of that is beside the point and it doesn't matter either if Lawson worked for Petiver, a London pharmacist, or if he was a great botanist or a great naturalist or if he plagiarized information from another book for his book or if he lied about his education or even if he co-founded New Bern.

"More important are Lawson's powerful friends and their land swindle.

"Adam, if historians dug a little deeper you might accept several more of their conclusions that some still bicker over, that Lawson was just a petty thief when he was sued by Daniel for money he owed him. However, it is really an important clue about the swindle.

"Lawson was subpoenaed and an order issued for his arrest to make certain that he would appear in court. It happened just before the collapse of the government that closed the courts.

"Lawson had been commissioned as the Surveyor for Bath County by Daniel because Lawson agreed to pay Daniel one half of his surveying fees. Adam, back then Bath County was huge stretching from the Albemarle area, where Raleigh's explorers settled, all the way to the area around your hometown.

"Daniel sued when he discovered there had been many more surveys in 1704-1705 than Lawson had reported and realized that Lawson had failed to pay him his half of Lawson's surveying fees.

"Gale represents Lawson and in the court records Gale informs the court that Lawson confesses that in addition to the 20 surveys he had already reported to Daniel he had also made 39 additional surveys. The court ordered him to pay one-half of the surveyor's fees and all the money Daniel had paid to collect the debt.

"Or another conclusion held by some, that it is no big deal Lawson was sued for debts because it was a common occurrence for respectable people to be sued over debts in those days.

"Adam I really do not understand how they reach such illogical conclusions because the main thing is this, there was a whole lot more going on than surveys and they knew Landgrave Daniel was loyal to the Lords Proprietors. They could only report 20 surveys to Daniel that had legitimate grants of land from the Lords Proprietors and had to keep secret 39 surveys for stolen Indian lands and that is the real reason why Lawson could not pay Daniel.

"There were land swindles going on that had to be kept from Daniels, the Lords Proprietors, and England because they would not like it if they knew how the rascals were stealing and selling Indian's lands and keeping all of the money for themselves.

"Daniel wrote a letter about it to the Lords Proprietors and they demanded an immediate accounting for all of their land warrants and their money and that's when things really got dangerous.

"What the Lords Proprietors got instead was anarchy, Adam. The history books call it Cary's first rebellion. The same kind of drunken mobs are also in the southern part of Carolina. You can read about the rebellions in that 1705 pamphlet to England's House of Commons. I will not go into all of that, but if you want to know more, there are many other records in the Colonial and State Records kept at the University of North Carolina at Chapel Hill, Documenting the American South, telling all about it.

"What I do want to tell you about is what was going on in politics around here. Politics drives governments and votes are what politicians need to win the election so they can drive the government in the direction they want it to go.

"Back then about the only entertainment people had would be when politicians held rallies for the public at election time and they wanted their votes.

"Politicians were like rock stars are now at a concert. At first, there would be musicians and different people giving witty and funny presentations to warm up the crowd. As the day wore on the people feasted on the free meat that had been roasting all day and there would be plenty of free rum to drink.

"That is when the big politicians would give their speeches, like politicians still do today; when they want to whip-up the crowd with rallies and speeches to sway them to their way of thinking, turning them into an angry mob when it suits their plans.

"The government and religious officials who were still loyal to Carolina's Fundamental Constitution and to the Lords Proprietors and the Queen encountered violence and threats of death by the angry mobs shouting 'down with the landgraves...'

"Adam because it was a cleaver believable scheme, selling land they did not own to hundreds of duped planters, this turned into a lot more than a land swindle. It turned into a rebellion to save their heads by attempting to overthrow the Lords Proprietor and Carolina's Fundamental Constitution form of government. Remember the law said they would forfeit everything they owned and banished forever. However, for treason they could lose their heads.

"Nana do you believe that's all true?" asked Adam.

"I do Adam, the swindles are well documented but you can read all about it in the official Minutes of the Carolina General Assembly. In the 1711 Minutes of the Carolina General Assembly they accuse Cary, Moseley, Moseley's bookkeeper, and others of swindling the settlers and in the 1712 Minutes of the Carolina General Assembly they document the imaginary surveys, calling them 'Crimes and Misdemeanors', naming Cary, Moseley and the others as 'perpetrators of fraud for selling land without warrants and unlawfully collecting fees'. You know, running a real estate swindle.

"The victims had plenty of evidence, many of the documents and surveys have Lawson's name on them, and Lawson's name would have been listed with the others involved if he had been alive.

"It is a long document and I won't read it to you because I know you will banish it before I get past the first paragraph, but if anyone wants to know the facts they should read the complete transcript, of the official Minutes of the colonial Carolina General Assembly, which in the harshest words records what the rascals did, why they were convicted, and forbidden to hold any government office for a year among other things which included paying back the victims; and all of those real estate sales were made void.

"Adam, reading the colonial records, looking for clues why the Indians killed Lawson for revenge, is one of those times when you have to be prepared to accept the facts and forget what you had been led to believe by others. You have to keep an open mind when history reveals secrets, exposing the ugly truth."

Clues Lead To The Truth

"For the past four years I've been researching the history of New Bern. Starting before there were any colonies in America, when only Native Americans lived here, to the present.

"First focusing on the founding of Virginia by Raleigh and the grant of Carolina to the Lords Proprietors and the beginning of Carolina's history; then following Carolina's paper trails through the colonial records of Carolina, Virginia, Africa, Spain, England, and Switzerland, for a hundred years, from 1629 to 1729 when the king buys Carolina from seven of the Lords Proprietors.

"Only then does the true 'back-stories' unfold, revealing rascals and their swindles, and a lot of other important things.

"The first Carolina land swindle was discovered in 1629; just a few months after our Lords Proprietors received their Carolina grant. The Lords Proprietors had to ask for royal intervention before they could even settle their first colony in Carolina.

"That was not the last land swindle, before our Baron moved here there had already been several others. The land swindle that spells trouble for our Baron and almost destroys New Bern had been going on for about 10 years before the founding of New Bern.

"The Board of Trade of England, Virginia's Governors, and

Carolina's Lords Proprietors had received so many complaints from the Indians that the Lords Proprietors and the Queen grew suspicious and on several occasions they demanded an accounting of their land Grants and Warrants, and of their money, and a survey of the dividing line between Virginia and North Carolina.

"For instance, Thomas Pollock was North Carolina's largest land owner, and even though he wasn't one of the rascals involved in the swindle, he stole land from the Indians. Pollock himself, and Virginia's Governor Spotswood, both wrote several letters about how Pollock did it.

"In fact, in Volume 01, Pages 727-728, of the Colonial, and States Records housed at the University of North Carolina at Chapel Hill, you can read a letter Pollock wrote on May 27, 1710 to John Lawson confessing to it.

"He says he is writing as soon as he learned of Lawson's returning from London with the Palatines and Gale.

"Pollock tells Lawson the same story Governor Spotswood tells, Pollock confesses how he intimidated a whole village of the Maherine Indians, imprisoning the Indians for two days in the sweltering heat of summer with no food or drink. Pollock even ordered some of their cabins, furniture, food, and corn gardens destroyed to prove he was serious. That they had better leave if they knew what was good for them. The land they were on was now his.

"Destroying the Indian's food and corn garden was so serious and despicable that the starving Indians would never forgive or forget it.

"Pollock says he was writing Lawson because he's afraid that because of what he did some people blame him for the Indians uprising, and Pollock knew his enemies had written the Lords Proprietors about it.

"Pollock added that he didn't doubt that Lawson knew about the Lords Proprietors dismissing Cary and giving all the power of Administration of the government to the new President they had elected.

"That Lawson had been at his house in May 1709, when they discussed Cary's first rebellion in 1708, and since that time he had been living in Virginia because he was not willing to live under an illegal government and hoped Lawson knew of any order's or news for settling Carolina's government.

"Pollock's letter goes on to say that because of his oath of loyalty to the Lords Proprietors he had to obey President Glover's lawful orders and maintain the legitimate government of the Lords Proprietors.

"That he knew Lawson was aware of the opinions held by Moseley, Cary, and the Lords Proprietors and would be ever grateful if he would tell him, assuring him he would never reveal what he said.

"In other documents, Pollock tells about the meeting of the General Assembly where he relates the illegal acts of Moseley and Cary, when Cary refused to give up the government to President Glover, setting off Cary's first rebellion.

"Some historians have written that Cary's Rebellions were about religious and political freedoms, and it's clear they fall for the same ruse the rascals used to whip-up the mobs, because most of them had moved to America to escape religious persecution. However, when you take into consideration the rascals motives, their method of operations, and their actions you can also see what the Carolina General Assembly saw 'Crimes and Misdemeanors'.

"In those Minutes Carolina's General Assembly tells how Crimes and Misdemeanors were committed using fraudulent surveys, illegally taking up and selling land and collecting the money without following the required procedures according to the Fundamental Constitution of Carolina and the Lords Proprietors instructions.

"Because of the nature of land sales, it took several key people to pull the swindles off. On the one hand, you had to record surveys and give the buyer their documents requiring the stamp of Carolina's Great Seal and a survey plot map.

"On the other hand it had to have the Governor's signature.

"But not all of Carolina's officials were in on it, like the former Deputy Governor Daniel, who was loyal to the Lords Proprietors. Who was surprised to learn Lawson had cheated him out of 39 surveying fees, for surveys of land he did not know about yet each required his signature as Governor several times.

"It's about this time that Gale sues Lawson. Lawson had entered into a contract with Gale for animal furs and Gale paid him in advance, probably to pay Daniel. The fact that Lawson was unable to deliver the furs shows that Lawson's relationship with the Indians had deteriorated.

"By the end of 1708 there was no legitimate government and no courts. During the next several years, the rascals agitated the settlers with false rumors and there was just anarchy. Cary, Moseley, and the other rascals were running everything with an illegal government, but more importantly, they continued to steal and sell Indian lands. They have an ulterior motive, too. They need voters and only men who own land could vote.

"There's a lot of information you can easily find in other books all about that so I won't go into the details about Cary's rebellions and his refusing to give up being the Governor; and stealing North Carolina's state records and the Great Seal of North Carolina. None of that stops them from continuing their swindle, stealing, and selling Indian's land.

"As I said before, Carolina's stolen records and Seal were never found and interestingly some of Bath County's Court documents went missing too, including pages of the bound book that recorded land transactions. I was following a paper trail from information I learned reading court documents that had referred to a sale of 640 acres of land by Lawson and when I read the notice in the front of the book regarding the missing pages, I realized the missing pages were the records I was looking for.

"It was about this time, because of continuing complaints from the Maherine Indians about the actions of Carolina's surveyors, and in defiance of the Queens command, Virginia sent spies to watch the surveyors. In their reports to the Board of Trade of England, they confirm the Indians' complaints are true and they accuse Survey General Moseley and Deputy Surveyor General Lawson by name.

"Not only is Moseley a famous attorney he serves in Carolina's highest government positions and is a Deputy Lord Proprietor, they had the Great Seal of Carolina so it is no wonder that hundreds of people had faith in Moseley when they bought land from him. Most were ignorant, illiterate and only knew what the rascals told them and the reasons why the rascals got away with their swindle for such a long time.

"By 1710 the main thing about all of that chaos, as far as our Baron is concerned, is this: the Lords Proprietors, Moseley, Lawson, Pollock, Cary, Gale, England's Board of Trade and Virginia's Governor Spotswood, and many others, all knew about the swindles and the mobs shouting 'down with the landgraves', but none informed our Baron.

"Instead, our Baron was encouraged by the Lords Proprietors, who had required that a member of the John Ritter Company become a Landgrave, to undertake the settling of a colony with almost 800 people, leaving him to figure it all out for himself.

"They gave Hyde written instructions to treat the Indians well and that the best way to deal with the rebels was with gentleness, but Hyde was mostly in the dark too. It seems they were clearly counting on our Baron and his large number of settlers to give Governor Hyde their support, and bring the situation under control when they get here. The truth is they let them walk blindly into anarchy, chaos, and the beginnings of a terrible Indian war.

"I can see why, if our Baron and his settlers had known everything that had been going on they would all have moved to Virginia, instead of Carolina.

"Virginia's Governor Spotswood wrote to the Board of Trade of England, denouncing the Lords Proprietors for sending our Baron and the Palatines here and not helping them.

"One of the ministers of the Church of England wrote to the Bishop something like 'for God's sake send 20 pounds immediately…we are all starving to death'. Then he went on to say the Lords Proprietors had censured him for complaining in his previous letter to the Bishop but they would have everyone do what Lawson did, 'praise this worthless place…'

"The story about Cary's second Rebellion in 1710 is often told about in stories but sometimes it's obvious that not digging deep enough they miss important details and suggest they were fighting for noble causes.

"While that might be true for most of the people they instigated to rebel, it was not the reason the rascals lead them to revolt. Like today, when politicians tell voters what they want to hear in order to get their votes, or even turn them into angry mobs, for their own personal reasons.

"Oh, at first, I also believed some of those stories, but as I dug through the years and read hundreds of letters and documents the facts opened my eyes and I could see reality from a different perspective," Nana confessed.

"Deputy Governor Hyde, who was a relative of the Queen's and had been appointed and sent by the Lords Proprietors, and our Baron who was loyal to his sworn allegiance to the Queen and to the Lords Proprietors, sided with Hyde and he would never let his hundreds of fighting-age men join Cary's rebellion.

"That's the reason Cary wanted to kill both our Baron and Hyde. It's well documented, how Cary came to New Bern and his threats of violence intimidated the Swiss and Palatines to stay out of it and not side with Hyde.

"Cary not only attempted to kill our Baron and Governor Hyde himself he promised rewards to the hot-headed younger Tuscarora Indians if they went on the warpath and would throw in a bonus if they kidnapped Governor Hyde.

"That's sometimes discounted by a few historians, Adam, but it's true. Manipulators all across the country frequently got the Indians to do their dirty work and fight for them and considered it a plus if Indians died because they wanted to get them out of the way. They even had a saying about it, 'The only good Indian was a dead Indian.'

"A Palatine woman and her young son were at Captain William Brice's when she heard the rascals' plotting to kill our Baron. She rowed a boat across the Trent River to Union Point to warn our Baron so when Brice and his men came to his cabin our Baron was ready and foiled their kidnapping plot.

"Brice was the one who lead his men to attack a Pamlico Indian village. They shoved a spit through the body of one of the Bay River chiefs and roasted him alive, in order to incite the local Indians into going on the warpath. So do not doubt for a moment that given the chance Brice would have kidnapped and killed our Baron.

"Adam, a lot of the evidence was not missing because the victims had their plot maps and other documents proving the land swindle.

"Those court documents from the trials and some of the Minutes of North Carolina's General Assembly I already told you about hold important clues documenting the problems with the titles to the land, complaints about incorrect surveys, overlapping surveys and other surveying problems. Some complained they had imaginary surveys because no surveyors ever set foot on their land yet they still received a plot maps from Lawson.

"I will tell you a little riddle I thought of Adam. Earth's latitude and longitude lines are not imaginary lines; even though you cannot see them, survey instruments can locate them.

"The riddle then is this: When does moving an imaginary boundary line add more land? Answer, when it's a swindle because you can't stretch land."

"I made up a riddle too. Nana, when is the round earth really flat?"

"Umm, when Columbus was a boy your age?" guessed Nana.

"No Nana, the round earth is flat when it's a map."

"That is a good riddle Adam let's put it in our book, okay?"

"Okay and I liked your riddle Nana."

"Thanks," Nana replied then added, "But this is deadly serious Adam. Back then, you could lose your head for treason, so the rascals will not go down without a fight and they fight dirty. They don't care who they hurt, they only care about saving their own necks."

Our Baron Did Not Have A Clue

"When we focus on stories about our Baron and Lawson and what really was going on around your hometown then it seems as if our Baron had many options, all of them bad.

"Today, in addition to the restored colonial records there's plenty of related documents available on the internet, including Bath County court documents, survey maps, letters, and diaries. Where we find the names of Carolina's key government officials and we can see on document after document the names of those involved like Moseley, Cary, Gale, and Lawson, sometimes as principles and sometimes as witnesses. You know Adam, where we can see the rascals at work.

"Adam, do not think that Lawson did not know what was going on during the eleven years he lived and worked in Carolina, but more to the point, if he did not like what was going on, he did not have to stay and continue to survey and steal Indian's land.

"Lawson's steady advancement and the important government positions he held, as well as his continuous and close association with Cary, Gale, and Moseley altogether prove, beyond a doubt, that Lawson was an important and willing participant when he joined the rascals in their swindle and he benefited greatly from it, acquiring money, land, and power for himself.

"Adam, it's not hard to understand what an important job a surveyor had. The Lords Proprietors required that every sale of land had to have a recorded survey and recorded land surveys are still required today.

"I believe greed, for money and power, were the rascal's motives. The swindlers made money from fees all along the process, from the governor on down to the surveyors. Of course, there would also be fees owed to the attorneys, who create the documents required to sell the land and fees to the Registrar and the Clerk of Court.

"Their big land swindle is almost the perfect crime because England was so far away so they are able to get away with it for a very long time, except for Lawson, who was punished by the Indians and who died just before the swindle falls apart.

"I think that is probably why Gale sued to get hold of Lawson's hair trunk when he learned some of Lawson's papers were inside.

"Some have the opinion there never was a hair trunk, but I think that is nonsense; because Gale sued Lawson's child and wife for the trunk, claiming to be Lawson's biggest creditor and demanded in court records that the trunk be given to him instead of Lawson's heirs because he said Lawson died owing him money.

"When you think about it, a hair trunk with some used wigs could hardly have been worth anything by themselves and an important, wealthy attorney like Gale and who was Carolina's Chief Justice, would not need Lawson's used wigs. Gale wanted to make certain that if there were any writings of Lawson's he would get them because not knowing what the writings were he was afraid they might incriminate him if they fell into the wrong hands.

"As you read through the years of documents, you can see that in the beginning the people didn't know what was really going on. As you read on, the pieces start to come together exposing the truth, and you start getting a clearer and bigger picture because you can see years and years of the rascal's actions all at once. The story unfolds right before your eyes and you know the future. You know what is going to happen to the Indians, Lawson, our Baron, and to New Bern.

"You can see the rascal's lies, and you can see people catching on, and you can see why the Indians got mad, wanted revenge, and tortured Lawson to death, and how the Golden Rule saved our Baron.

"The Neusiok Chief did not forget that our Baron always treated them fairly and had paid them for Chatooka when our Baron and Lawson were being held prisoners. The Neusiok Chief vouched for our Baron at that same council where all of those Chiefs remembered that Lawson surveyed apart their lands and refusing to forgive him, they condemned Lawson to death.

"Early on, Virginia's Governor uncovers the swindle, somewhat, causing an investigation by the Queen and the Lords Proprietors, with the result that both forbid the sale of any land along the border between Virginia and Carolina until a survey could determine the true location of the dividing line.

"Which doesn't happen, it drags on from 1700-1729, because governors, kings, and queens died, wars and tragedy happened, and other factors, including many well documented efforts to deliberate delay the survey by Moseley and Lawson.

"Especially Moseley, even after Lawson died he was still trying to prevent the survey in 1729. The point being he never stopped trying to prevent the true dividing-line to be located on the ground for almost 30 years. Which I believe is clue enough, all by its self, since he was Carolina's Surveyor General it was his job and he had orders from both the Crown and the Lords Proprietors to survey the dividing line on the ground, but there are more clues.

"By 1729 there were so many people living in Carolina along the border with Virginia, and who were not paying rents, and still no survey of the dividing line, causing King George III to buy Carolina just to settle the dispute of whether the quit rents belonged to the King or to the Lords Proprietors.

"The king paid seven of the Lords Proprietors 2,500 pounds each and forgave them from owing all the years of missing quit rents, of course the Lords Proprietors never received their shares either or they would not have gotten off so easily. Only Lord Beaufort held on to his 1/8 share; leaving it to his heirs, of course he was no longer a Lord Proprietor.

"Making Carolina a royal colony like Virginia meant that now Carolinians were the king's tenants not the Lords Proprietors but they were still tenants, Adam.

"It took months to communicate between Carolina and England, relying on slow ships to deliver documents and lucky mail, being lucky if it reached its destination. Protected from interception only by honesty, wax seals, and occasionally protected by superstition with an evil eye symbol.

"The rascals were the ones in control, powerful and ruthless in Carolina and in England master manipulators, pulling the wool over the eyes of the Lords Proprietors. Creating an illusion of being trustworthy, they were bold and unafraid, robbing the Lords Proprietors right under their noses for years.

"But never in a million years could I have imagined these true stories and how the consequences would cause so much trouble for so many people and for so many years, as well as what happened to our Baron because of that rascally gang.

"Adam, the thing about history is this: history takes time and it is made of stories about decisions made and their intended and unintended consequences, for good or bad. Sometimes it is hard to tell which is which when everything is happening, that is when the big picture and time becomes important.

"Lawson had been involved in Carolina's history for about eight years by the time he meets our Baron in1709.

"Lawson's journey started from Charleston, South Carolina in December 1700, taking him about two months, traveling about nine miles a day through Carolina's vast and dangerous wilderness before reaching his destination. Traveling about 550 miles not the 1,000 miles he claims.

"Which is still an awesome accomplishment, but it was thanks to the Indians, who welcomed, guided, and fed him that Lawson's journey across Carolina was possible. Lawson and his Indian guide Eno Will reached Richard Smith's plantation on the Pamlico River in February of 1701.

"Bath County was established in 1696, and in 1704 David Perkins, one of Carolina's four largest landowners, transferred about 60 acres of his property to Lawson, Joel Martin, and Simon Alderson for Bath Town.

"By March 8, 1705, Lawson had surveyed Bath Town into 71 lots, becoming North Carolina's first incorporated town.

"Lawson, Martin, and Nicholas Daw, another of the four largest landowners, became Bath's first commissioners, which is why they created Bath. Being government officials gave cleaver men power and opportunities. Now, they can record the land transactions in Bath Town, which is under their control.

"September 26, 1706 Lawson buys two of the most desirable waterfront lots to build his house located on the point of waterfront land, looking much like Union Point where our Baron had his cabin.

"Remember, for the first couple of years Lawson is constantly at work as a surveyor and by 1704 he was appointed the Surveyor of Bath County by Governor Daniels and Surveyor General Moseley appointed him his Deputy Surveyor of Carolina in 1705.

"Lawson builds his house in Bath and is surveying plantations around Chatooka and builds his cabin on Lawson Creek.

"January 1706 to August 1708, Lawson serves as Clerk of Court and Public Registrar of Pampticough Precinct, in Bath County; a very lucrative position back then, earning him fees on all transactions, which consists mainly of recording real estate documents.

"April 15, 1707 Lawson becomes a father.

"By 1708, Queen Anne once again insists on a ground survey of the Virginia border with Carolina, therefore Virginia is pressing Carolina to survey the dividing-line.

"Early in 1708 William Lord Craven becomes Lord Palatine and Lawson and Mosley travel to England to make certain the Lords Proprietors appoint them both to be Carolina's Commissioners, overseeing the dividing-line survey.

"Lawson is sued, for the survey money he owes Daniel and misses a meeting with Moseley and the Virginia surveyors.

"Daniel informs the Lords Proprietors of the swindle; Carolina's Lords Proprietors demand an accounting of all of their land warrants and the payment of their rent monies, which sets off Cary's first rebellion, causing the collapse of the Lords Proprietors' government and closes the courts. This is when Lawson makes out his Will; he knows they could all lose their heads.

"1709 there are twelve houses in Bath Town when Lawson goes to London to publish his book, which he dedicates to the Lords Proprietors and proudly adds his title, Surveyor General, on the cover and sells a copy of his map to the Lords Proprietors for 20 pounds.

"In April 28, 1709 Franz Luis Michel tries to get a grant of land for the Ritter Company from the Lords Proprietors. They tell him that first he needs one of his partners in the Ritter Company to purchase 5,000 acres and the title Landgrave.

"Several years earlier, Michel, and the John Ritter Company

had tried to get a grant of land that would be without any ties to England, basically trying to start their own country. Of course, the Lords Proprietors refused.

"While in London, Lawson meets up with Michel who is still there trying to get a land grant from the Lord Proprietors for the George Ritter Company. In his journal, Lawson tells about first meeting Michel in Carolina.

"Adam, it's about this time that our Baron's term as lieutenant-governor of Yverdon, Switzerland ended and he had recently moved back to Bern looking for his next career move.

"Our Baron said he remained skeptical of the Ritter Company's proposal at first until Michel introduced him to Carolina's Surveyor General Lawson, who vouches for Michel.

"It probably seemed like a windfall for Lawson because all of a sudden, with our Baron involved as Landgrave, almost eight hundred immigrants are moving to Carolina, which means Surveyor General Lawson will be making a whole lot of money.

"Our Baron thought he could see that Lawson's business opportunities were the reason he thought Lawson manipulated him into buying Chatooka, but there were more important reasons. Our poor Baron and his tenants in many ways were innocent-by-standers who come upon chaos. Not pretend chaos either Adam, people were really dying.

"If Lawson and Michel had not interfered, talking our Baron into becoming the required Landgrave, there's no doubt our Baron would have had a very different American adventure.

"Even today, some try to credit Lawson with founding New Bern by saying he was the one that brought the main body of settlers here and that he was the one who laid out New Bern.

"Some have even blamed the Tuscarora Indian War on our Baron, because he paid the Neusiok Indians for Chatooka with powder and shot instead of running them off like Lawson advised and Michel tried to do. They even dismiss with a few words the charge against Lawson of stealing Indian lands, proving they do not know, or do not understand the back-story that drove the Indians to seek revenge against Lawson.

"New Bern was founded because our Baron agreed to become a Carolina Landgrave and we saw the map he made, laying out New Bern with the locations of his tenants plantations. He even wrote about how he selected the locations for the streets and that he participated in surveying New Bern.

"Lawson was not interested in our Baron's colony getting off to a good start Adam, his interest was with that 'rascally gang' our Baron wrote about, and he didn't layout New Bern nor settle the Palatines on their own land as he was instructed by our Baron before they left England.

"Lawson took them to his place and had them clearing out his own land because he had lied about there not being any Indians in the way. There's no doubt he knew that the Neusiok Indian village Chatooka was occupying the land sold to our Baron for his colony and even wrote about the village in his book.

"Some claim that Carolina's Fundamental Constitution was not in effect but they ignore the fact that it was only because of it that was our Baron was made a member of Carolina's royalty, as a Landgrave, and that he had the right and the obligation to mortgage the land, and to go to England and Switzerland for help. God knows there was no help to be gotten here."

"Nana, if our Baron had moved to Virginia I'm certain that the queen would have helped him," declared Adam.

"And I'm certain that our Baron would not have moved to Carolina to be a Carolina Landgrave and he would not have paid the Indians powder and shot for Chatooka if he really knew what was going on," decided Adam.

"Adam your points have given us our final two clues proving our Baron didn't have a clue about 'who was who and what was what'.

"We will never understand why disasters and tragedies happen, Adam, but we learned that our Baron tried his best in a difficult and unsatisfactory situation and we learned why we should be proud such an excellent adventurer founded your hometown on his American adventure, even if he did have to leave it in shambles.

"I hope we have cleared away the smears some have put upon our Baron's name. What do you think?"

THE END

Photo Album: Wishing You Were Here With Me Walking in the Footsteps of History

2007, Adam, with a "devilish" twinkle in his eye, as he tells Nana his plans for a "scary adventure with real pirates," that will give her "endless nightmares"

2007, Adam and Nana feeding the carriage horse an apple, at the carriage stop on Middle Street, New Bern, NC

2007, Adam, his brother Nelson, and Nana in the carriage, ready for a Christmas Eve carriage ride through historic New Bern, NC

2008, Adam is posing for a photo of him with the bust, but before Adam learned that a picture of one of Baron deGraffenried's relatives was use to sculpt the bust

2009, Adam posing beside the sign informing visitors they need a ticket in order to pass through the front gate to the Governor's Palace. (All money stays in New Bern, for the Tryon Palace Commission to operate the historic sites in its care

2009, Adam posing for an illustration that will be featured on one of his adventure into history maps

2009, Adam posing at top of a knoll overlooking Fort Macon State Park, featuring a warning sign for his adventure into history photo album, prompting Nana to yell at him, "Don't fall into the fort!"

2009, Adam posing beside a warning sign at the entrance path leading to Fort Macon State Park, for his adventure into history photo album

Left, Adam's Aunt "Goddess" Donna, standing beside
Adam's Mom, Wanda (AKA "Aunt Kitty Cat")

2010, Adam, on New Bern's award winning Middle Street, posing   under banners celebrating New Bern's 300th birthday

2011, Adam, downtown New Bern, posing beside his favorite
wooden statue, at Bear Plaza on Middle Street, so that the bear
is reflected in the store's window

Adam observing a blacksmith at work, during the 20011 Civil War reenactment at Union Point Park

Adam's great-grandfather, Donald Nunley, who is holding his granddaughter, Starr

April 1, 2011, Adam is posing in front of the NC History
Center for his photo album

Part 3: FOR THOSE WHO WANT TO FOLLOW CLUES AND DIG DEEPER

Web Sites: Using clues he left behind, follow Adam's footsteps into history online. Our list includes websites offering free, fun, educational activities and North Carolina curriculum lesson plans for all grades

http://www.royal.gov.uk/Home.aspx
http://www.englishmonarchs.co.uk/stuart8.htm
http://avalon.law.yale.edu/16th_century/raleigh.asp
http://www.schoolhistory.co.uk/lessons/armada/whywar.htm
http://www.nationalarchives.gov.uk/
http://www.historylearningsite.co.uk
http://www.degraffenreid.org
http://statelibrary.ncdcr.gov/nc/ncsites
http://www.nps.gov/history/history/online
http://www.ecu.edu/cs-lib/ncc/index
http://docsouth.unc.edu/nc/barlowe/barlowe.html
http://www.patc.us/history/native/michel2.html
http://kids.mapzones.com
http://www.kidinfo.com/american_history/colonization roanoke
http://www.learnnc.org
http://teachnet-lab.org/miami/2004/linero2/4religion%20golden%20rule.htm
http://www.friendsofblairmountain.org
http://www.marines.mil/unit/mcascherrypoint

Books: Our list of highly recommended books
In addition to regular library services, many of the
recommended books are available 24-7 on NC LIVE (nclive.
org) to any North Carolina resident with Internet access and
a valid NC library card. Contact your local library for the
internet code to open the portal first.

Through Indian Eyes: The Untold Story Of Native American
Peoples
Author: Reader's Digest
Publisher: Reader's Digest Association Pleasantville, NY:, c
1995. 400 p
ISBN:089577819X

The History Of New Bern And Craven County, NC
Author: by Watson, Alan D
Publisher: New Bern Craven County, NC: Tryon Palace
Commission, c 1987. 746 p.
Craven-Pamlico-Carteret Regional Library, Kellenberger
Room: R NC 975.6192 W,

A New Bern Album
Author: Green III, John B.
Publisher: New Bern: Tryon Palace Commission, ©1985.
Craven-Pamlico-Carteret Regional Library, Call #: NC
975.6192 G,

The De Graffenried Family Scrap Book
Author: de Graffenried, Thomas P.
Publisher: The University of VA Press, Charlottesville, VA,
1958 Not Copyrighted.
Craven-Pamlico-Carteret Regional Library, NC 929.2. Library
of Congress CS71.G738 929.2

The History of The deGraffenried Family from 1191 A.D. to 1925

Author: deGraffenried, Thomas P.

Published by the Author: The Vail-Ballou Press, Binghamton, and New York, 1925

"Not Copyrighted, Permission is given to republish the whole or any part of this work."

WorldCat Libraries: 49796870

Craven-Pamlico-Carteret Regional Library

The History And Romance Of Exploration Told With Pictures

Author: Seymour Gates Pond; Captions by Shepard Rifkin

Publisher: Cooper Square Publishers, Inc.

Library of Congress Catalog Card Number 65-17180 G 80.P67

The Tuscarora

Author: Witt, Shirley Hill

Publication: New York, Crowell-Collier Press 1972.

Craven-Pamlico-Carteret Regional Library, Call #: J970.3 W

History Of The Choctaw, Chickasaw, And Natchez Indians.

Author: Cushman, H. B. b. 1822.; Debo, Angie,

Publication: Norman : University of Oklahoma Press, 1999

Internet Resource Computer File: www.netLibrary.com

Libraries Worldwide: 843

A New Voyage To Carolina

Author: Lawson, John

Publisher: Chapel Hill [N.C.] : University of North Carolina Press ©1967.

Craven-Pamlico-Carteret Regional Library 917.56

Blackbeard's Last Fight
Author: Kinnel, Eric A, Fisher; Leonard, Everett
Publisher: NY: Farrar, Straus, and Geroux 2006
WorldCat Libraries: NCJKIM